IRISH STEAM

IRISH STEAM

A Twenty-year Survey, 1920–1939

O. S. NOCK
BSc, CEng, FICE, FIMechE

DAVID & CHARLES
Newton Abbot   London   North Pomfret

British Library Cataloguing in Publication Data

Nock, O.S.
  Irish steam: a twenty-year survey, 1920–1939
  1. Locomotives—Ireland—History—20th century
  I. Title
  625.2'61'09415   TJ603.4.I/

  ISBN 0-7153-7961-5

Typeset by Northern Phototypesetting Co, Bolton
and printed in Great Britain
by Biddles Limited, Martyr Road, Guildford
for David & Charles (Publishers) Limited
Brunel House   Newton Abbot   Devon

Published in the United States of America
by David & Charles Inc
North Pomfret   Vermont 05053   USA

Contents

Preface		7
1	The Railway Scene in 1920	11
2	Irish Locomotive Men	25
3	Great Southern & Western: 1920–1924	37
4	Midland Great Western: Most Irish of railways	48
5	First Thoughts on the Narrow Gauge: Into the deep south and west	63
6	Great Northern: 1920–1930	77
7	Belfast & County Down: A railway in decline	93
8	Northern Counties Committee: Compounds to Superheater 4–4–0s	102
9	Narrow Gauge in the north-west and north	115
10	Dublin & South Eastern	129
11	Rationalisation on the GSR	144
12	Great Northern: Compounds and Caledonian Blue	158
13	NCC: The Speir Effect	174
14	Great Southern: Climax of the Queens	188
Index		205

Preface

When David St J. Thomas asked me to add a volume on Irish Steam to those I had contributed in a similar vein on the four British main line companies in the Grouping era, I welcomed the opportunities it promised of reviving memories of what had been a very enjoyable series of excursions in the 1930s. When I first crossed the water, things had settled down after the Civil War; but at the same time I would imagine that there were very few people outside Ireland who fully realised the extent of the devastation and damage to railways that had been wrought in those tragic years. I had become acquainted with one aspect of it through my signalling work, when the invention of the hand-generator system of providing power for long-distance signal and point operation obviated the need for replacing signalboxes that had been destroyed. A notable example was that of Killarney Junction, on the main line just south of Mallow.

I should explain at the outset that this book makes no attempt to provide a complete record of all locomotives in service in the 1920–1940 period, nor yet an exhaustive survey of all the Irish railways. That would have been impossible within the parameters set out for me. I have, though, provided a broad picture, emphasising the more significant locomotive designs that were then in traffic and the way they performed in service, based very largely on my own personal experiences and note-taking at the time. I recall many good friends who made my Irish journeys most enjoyable; many have now passed on. One who I used to meet for lunch from time to time, was R. Bagwell. He was the son of a former General Manager of the Great Northern of Ireland. He was then Chief Passenger Trains Clerk in the office of the Divisional Superintendent of Operation on the LMS at Crewe, though himself based at Euston. His fund of reminiscence was limitless. Another LMS man, and a stop-watcher of wide experience in Ireland, was J. Macartney Robbins, a frequent contributor of fine photographs to *The*

NARROW GAUGE RAILWAYS

1   LONDONDERRY & LOUGH SWILLY
2   COUNTY DONEGAL JT.
3   BALLYCASTLE
4   BALLYMENA-CUSHENDALL AND REDBAY
5   BALLYMENA-LARNE
6   CASTLEDERG-VICTORIA BRIDGE
7   CAVAN & LEITRIM
8   CLOGHER VALLEY
9   DUBLIN-LUCAN
10 WEST CLARE
11 TRALEE & DINGLE
12 SCHULL & SKIBBEREEN
13 CORK & MUSKERRY
14 CORK, BLACKROCK & PASSAGE
15 GIANTS CAUSEWAY & PORTRUSH TRAMWAY
16 PORTSTEWART TRAMWAY
17 LISTOWEL & BALLYBUNION (Monorail)

———————   OTHER RAILWAYS (5' 3"GAUGE)

Railway Magazine. My numerous contacts on the NCC are mentioned at many points in the text; in addition to Major Speir, two high officers that I also had the pleasure of meeting were G. B. Howden, Chief Engineer and later General Manager of the Great Northern, and Edgar Bredin, Chief Mechanical Engineer of the Great Southern.

Howden I met in amusing and somewhat intimidating circumstances, when he had become General Manager. I had been riding on the footplate of one of the 170 Class 4-4-0s from Dublin, but having a business engagement immediately on arrival in Belfast decided to finish riding at Goraghwood to give me time to clean-up. I returned to my compartment to find Howden had joined the train at Dundalk, and he greeted his overalled fellow passenger cordially! Just after Christmas 1947 I had the honour of lecturing to the Royal Dublin Society on locomotive development, and I was delighted that Bredin and his wife were in the audience. Afterwards they came to a little gathering in the secretary's office, and Mrs Bredin told me a great story about *Maeve*. At the official residence at Inchicore they had a housemaid who was an enthusiastic locomotive 'spotter', and apparently she was very upset when for some reason it was decreed that *Maeve*, like other locomotives, should take rear-end banking assistance out of Kingsbridge station in Dublin. One morning, when they were at breakfast, this girl burst most unceremoniously into the dining room and could barely speak for excitement. Apparently the Cork Mail had just gone up the bank, with *Maeve* at its head, and in such style that the banker could not keep up, and was vainly puffing away for all it was worth about a coach length clear of the last vehicle!

I am much indebted to the writings of the late H. Fayle, which have graced the columns of *The Locomotive*, and *The Railway Magazine*, and to my great friends Ivo Peters and W. A. Camwell for much valuable information and photographs. Lastly, I am grateful to members of the Irish Railway Record Society for help on certain points of history.

O. S. Nock, July 1981

Batheaston, Bath.

CHAPTER 1

The Railway Scene in 1920

Until 1920 all Ireland was a part of the United Kingdom, but it would be entirely wrong to suggest that her railways were modelled on British lines. Apart from the question of rail gauge, the railways of both Great Britain and Ireland grew up together, with close interchange of ideas and personnel, and subject to the same statutory regulations, as required by successive Acts of Parliament passed at Westminster and to invigilation by Inspecting Officers of the Board of Trade. These regulations, of course, applied only to the broad gauge lines. The narrow gauge were in a group quite apart, and subject to the requirements of a series of Light Railway Acts. But the fact that the British and Irish main line railways grew up together, and under a code of practice that we like to think was the most stringent and efficient in the world, inevitably tends to make the British and Irish railways regarded in the same context, and to have caused surprise to visitors from Great Britain in days before 1920 to find how different the Irish were, in so many ways.

To appreciate reasons for the differences one must look first at some purely statistical points. First, there is the simple fact of population. The whole of Ireland, in the 1920s, south and north together and including such a large industrial city as Belfast, did not account for much more than half the population of London; and while there had grown up a moderate degree of business travel daily between Belfast and the capital city of Dublin, there was nothing comparable to demand frequent and rapid passenger services to the historic cities of the south and west: Waterford, Cork, Limerick, and Londonderry. There were no indigenous mineral resources, and the only traffic in that respect lay in the haulage of locomotive coal, imported either from England, Scotland, or Wales. This latter of course brought no revenue, unless it was being hauled for another company. As all the larger railways of Ireland ran either into Dublin or Belfast

11

there would be precious little of it for others. The revenue earning business in 'goods' came from dairy and agricultural traffic, and from livestock.

The very limited extent of the six major railways of Ireland, in 1920, can be appreciated from the route mileage worked over, thus,

Belfast & County Down	(BCDR)	80
Dublin & South Eastern	(DSER)	160
Great Northern	(GNR(I))	560
Great Southern & Western	(GS&WR)	1121
Midland Great Western	(MGWR)	538
Northern Counties Committee	(NCC)	263

The GS&WR had in 1901 taken-over the rather remarkable Waterford, Limerick & Western Railway which, believe it or not, had a main line no less than 222 miles long! It extended from Waterford via Clonmel, Tipperary, Limerick, up to Sligo, with a lengthy branch down to Tralee. With this latter, and other branches, it contributed 350 miles to the total of 1121 shown above for the GS&WR in 1920. To operate the total mileage of 2722, there were no more than about 820 locomotives on the broad (5ft 3in) gauge in all Ireland. Such figures, with one locomotive for every three miles of track, make a striking comparison with those of one English railway, the London & North Western, with roughly one locomotive for every mile of the 3038 over which it worked.

Despite the lack of heavy traffic and sparsity of population in most of the country served, the Irish railways were well and profitably managed. The relatively poor results from the Dublin & South Eastern could be attributed in some degree to the heavy cost of protective works against damage from the sea on the coastal section between Bray and Wicklow. The following were the dividends paid on the ordinary stock at the end of 1912:

	percent
Belfast & County Down	7
Dublin & South Eastern	1
Great Northern	$5\frac{1}{2}$
Great Southern & Western	5
Midland Great Western	3

The results from the Northern Counties Committee of the Midland Railway were not quoted separately from those of the parent company. As in Great Britain it was dividends similar to these that formed the basis of the compensation paid to shareholders during the period of Government control during the World War I.

From the end of the war in November 1918 these arrangements were continued for another two years 'with a view', as stated at the time, 'to affording time for the consideration and formulation of the policy to be pursued as to the future position'. This typically verbose piece of official jargon then applied to the British as well as to the Irish railways. In his interesting book *Fifty Years of Railway Life*, published in 1920, Joseph Tatlow, General Manager, and later Director of the Midland Great Western Railway succinctly sums-up the likely prospects that were to follow:

This arrangement, temporary in its nature, provides as is pretty generally known, that during its continuance, the railway companies shall be guaranteed the same net income as they earned in the year preceeding the war, *viz*, 1913. So far so good. But two years will quickly pass; and what then? It is also generally known that the Government control of the railways, during the war and since, has resulted in enormous additions to the working expenses. Perhaps these additions were inevitable. The cost of coal, and of all materials used in the working of railways, advanced by leaps and bounds; but the biggest increase has been in the wages bill. The Government granted these increases of wages, and also conceded shorter hours of labour, involving an immensity of expense, on their own responsibility, without consultation with the Irish railway companies. Upon the Irish railway companies, for the present position of affairs no responsibility, therefore, rests. Again I say, the course which the Government adopted was, perhaps, inevitable. They had to win the war. Labour was clamorous and insistent, and serious trouble threatened. High reasons of State may be presumed to have dictated the Government policy. Anyhow the thing is done, and the hard fact remains that the Irish railways have been brought to such a financial condition that, if they were handed back to the companies, many of them not only could not pay any dividends but would be unable to meet their fixed charges whilst some would not be able to even pay their working expenses.

Despite the generally satisfactory dividend position, which reflected upon good management, the Irish railways had, somewhat characteristically, been severely attacked in the early 1900s for inefficient service, and overcharging in respect of freight rates; but while it is true that passenger train speeds, even on the main lines of the Great Northern and GS&W Railways were far below the best English standards, those who criticised were playing the time-honoured game of 'knocking' the railways, without having the slightest need of accelerated service themselves for business or any other reasons. The service in pre-war years had been perfectly adequate for a rural community, and the overall average speeds of the best trains on the Dublin–Belfast and Dublin–Cork runs of little over 45mph were all that circumstances required. It is remarkable however to note the extent to which the fastest express train services were based on what could be termed the 'English connection', right down to the outbreak of the *second* World War, namely the arrival and departure of the night mail steamers to and from Holyhead, at Kingstown. There were through trains for Belfast, Cork, Galway and Waterford, which on the incoming service awaited the arrival of the steamer in the event of late running.

The loads of the express trains were mostly light by English standards. It was not often that a train of more than 300 tons was seen, even in wartime conditions. The Great Northern, Midland Great Western, and GS&WR lines all included sections of heavy grading, but except on the Great Northern piloting was frequently resorted to, even if for no more than short sections. Both ends of the Dublin–Cork main line included bad starts out of the terminus, and with heavy southbound trains the pilots were taken as far as Kildare. Northbound from Cork the pilot usually was detached at Blarney. There is one very heavy bank on the main line to Galway, about six miles west of Ballinasloe, $2\frac{1}{2}$ miles at 1 in 60, ending a mile before Woodlawn; but I have never seen any detailed timings on this route west of Mullingar, beyond which all trains then, as now, called at most intermediate stations. Even on the Great Northern main line, with gradients up to a maximum of 1 in 100 only in climbing the mountain section north of Dundalk, the timings were relatively easy. On the four sections usually run non-stop, Dublin to Drogheda, thence to Dundalk, Portadown and Belfast, for distances of $31\frac{1}{2}$,

$22\frac{1}{2}$, $33\frac{1}{4}$, and 25 miles the fastest times prior to 1920 were 38, 28, 43, and 29 minutes.

Until 1916 there were no passenger locomotives larger than the 4-4-0, and the great majority of these were non-superheated. As the following summary shows, there were not all that many of these:

Railway	*4–4–0*	*2–4–0*	*0–4–2*
Dublin & South Eastern	6	5	8
Great Northern	75	9	–
Great Southern & Western	85	12	–
Midland Great Western	22	32	–
Northern Counties Committee	24	10	–

In addition to the above I may add that the Belfast & County Down had four locomotives of the 2-4-0 type, but its busy commuter service out of Belfast was worked almost entirely by 4-4-2 tank engines. Superheaters were first introduced on Irish locomotives in 1911 when Charles Clifford of the Great Northern included them in the equipment of some new 4-4-0 and 0-6-0 locomotives put into service that year. He used the Phoenix type, which entailed an extended smokebox with the chimney right out in front. It gave the locomotives a horribly mis-shapen look, which was strange, because until then Clifford's engines, particularly his 4-4-0s, were to my mind the most beautifully proportioned of any in Ireland. This was Clifford's last throw, and as soon as Glover had succeeded him he immediately began building superheater 4-4-0s of quite orthodox appearance, using the Schmidt apparatus. In the same year of 1913 R.E.L. Maunsell produced the first superheater 4-4-0 for the GS&WR, a prototype that proved to be no more than a 'one-off', while in the following year Bowman Malcolm on the NCC produced his first non-compound engine since 1876, also a superheater 4-4-0.

The way in which senior officers of the locomotive departments moved between British and Irish companies will be referred in more detail in the next chapter, but the extent to which some of the Irish works based their operations on contemporary practice of one or another of the more famous English establishments was remarkable, even down to quite small details. There was perhaps no more striking example than that of Inchicore, in its many likenesses to Crewe. In purely superficial matters such as locomotive livery and the type of numberplates this was immediately apparent, though in another respect there was a striking difference. The Great Southern & Western stood apart from most of the Irish railways in having only a very few named engines, at a time when most of the others named not only their express, but also their goods, and local passenger tank engines. So far as numberplates were concerned the GS&WR in Alexander McDonnell's time was the originator of the cast type, in 1873. In England the LNWR copied them a few years later, and they became standard at Crewe. Until about 1902 the locomotive colour was similar to the so-called 'invisible green' of the Belfast & Northern Counties, after which the style adopted was almost exactly the same as the 'blackberry black' of the LNWR.

In 1920 the mail trains of the Great Southern & Western were still running through to Queenstown – Cobh, as it subsequently became. The express locomotives worked through over the $177\frac{1}{4}$ miles from Dublin (Kingsbridge). Queenstown was at that time still a trans-Atlantic packet station of some importance, though with the transfer of the prestige Cunard and White Star sailings from Liverpool to Southampton, Queenstown was no longer concerned with the principal American mails. Before this there had been a substantial time saving to be made by landing the inward-bound mails at Queenstown by tender and conveying them thence to English destinations via the GS&WR, Kingstown (Dun Laoghaire), and Holyhead. If the arrival of the steamer at Queenstown did not connect conveniently with the time of the regular Irish Mail service the mails were taken to Dublin North Wall, instead of Kingstown, and taken forward by special boat and train provided by the London & North Western Railway.

Plate 1(a) GSWR McDonnell type 0–6–0 introduced 1867. No 192 was one of the last to be built to this famous design in 1898, and not scrapped until 1956 (*L&GRP*)
(b) MGW 4–4–0 No 544 (formerly No 11 *Erin-go-Bragh*), entering Broadstone, Dublin, with a train from Sligo. The locomotive was scrapped in 1955. (*L&GRP*)
(c) GSWR four-cylinder 4–6–0 No 405 of Watson design, one of the batch built in 1923 by Armstrong Whitworth & Co. (*L&GRP*)

At one time according to the public timetables the special American mails, twice weekly to connect with outward-bound steamers, ran non-stop between Dublin and Cork, but actually there were stops presumably for water, at Portarlington and Limerick Junction. At the latter place, apparently, the only water columns were on the one long platform, with the result that even these special trains were subjected to the time-honoured draw-ahead and reversal manoevre to reach the platform. At Cork, it was not until the twentieth century that the express locomotives began working to Queenstown, and in earlier days it was usual to change them at Glanmire station and go forward with one of the Aspinall 0-4-4 tanks that worked all the local services. Right down to the outbreak of the World War II war there was quite a reasonable local train service between Cork and Cobh, as we should call it then.

The practice of landing eastbound passengers from America at Queenstown will always be remembered from the torpedoing of the great Cunarder *Lusitania* off the Old Head of Kinsale in May 1915 when she was almost within sight of Queenstown, where the tenders were putting out to meet her. The appalling loss of life in the sinking of that great liner brought home, more than anything else, the awful menace of the campaign of undersea attack being developed by the German naval command.

The timing of the mail trains, on all four trunk lines radiating from Dublin was dictated by the British Post Office, to provide 'return of post' service between towns and cities on the principal routes in both England and Ireland. The intervals between the arrival and departure of the English mails varied a little over the years, but after the establishment of the Irish Free State they were around 11.00am and 3.50pm in Cork; 10.55am and 3.15pm in Waterford; 11.00am and 3.30pm in Galway; 9.10am

Plate 2(a) GSWR 0-4-4 tank No 51 of McDonnell 1870 design, but continued by Aspinall. No 51 was built in 1883, scrapped 1934. (*L&GRP*)
(b) GSR: One of the earlier McDonnell 0-6-0s of the GS&WR, No 104 (built 1873) here shown as rebuilt with superheater, and remaining in service until 1965. (*L&GRP*)
(c) GS&WR: One of the later 4-4-2 tanks of the Aspinall type first introduced in 1894. The locomotive shown, No 320, was one of four built by R. Coey in 1901-2. They lasted until 1954. (*L&GRP*)

and 5.40pm in Belfast. Whether anyone in Galway, for example, ever bestirred himself to dash off a reply to a letter from England to catch the eastbound 'Limited Mail' at 3.30pm is another matter. But the facility was there, if the Post Office delivered the letters promptly. One nevertheless looks back rather wistfully to a time when such service was provided – when there were no such things as first- and second-class letters, and the whole job was done for three half-pence each way!

Except on the Great Northern even the mail trains did not exactly hurry. The average speeds revealed by the overall timings are indicative of the leisure of a generally rural community, thus:

Places	Miles	Minutes	Speed (mph)
Dublin-Cork	$165\frac{1}{2}$	235	42.3
Dublin-Waterford	$116\frac{1}{4}$	259	26.9
Dublin-Galway	$128\frac{3}{4}$	230	33.6

The Waterford Mail made a great number of intermediate stops, although carrying a restaurant car throughout. One could reach Waterford and Cork much earlier from London by using the Great Western service via Fishguard and Rosslare. The arrivals by this were 7.10am at Waterford, and 10.03am at Cork. The overall time from London was the same in the latter case as via Holyhead and Dublin. In Ireland the 6.10am from Rosslare Harbour took 233 minutes to cover the $134\frac{1}{4}$ miles to Cork, a not very exciting average speed of 34.6mph.

If the speeds run by the crack Irish express passenger trains were nothing to speak of, some of the coaching stock and the 4-4-0 locomotives were very handsome. It is true that by the end of the war the more distinguished locomotive liveries had given place to black, and the addition of superheating equipment was not improving the very handsome lines of the Great Northern and MGW classes, quite apart from the hideous effect of the experiments with the Phoenix type by Clifford on the Great Northern. The engineers on Irish railways certainly produced some curious external effects when introducing superheating, and on the MGWR in 1916 when modernising some of Cusack's beautiful Mercuric class, of 1902, W. H. Morton produced an extended smokebox in which the additional internal capacity was provided by a very deeply dished opening door. It was obviously a cheap way of obtaining the space required, but it was not beautiful!

At that time, and in perpetuity during the steam era, with no more than slight variations, the 'Limited Mail' was allowed 76 minutes in each direction for its non-stop run between Dublin (Broadstone) and Mullingar, $50\frac{1}{4}$ miles. The westbound run was decidedly the harder, because the first $5\frac{1}{2}$ miles is steeply adverse. After that the gradients, though having a rising tendency throughout, are not difficult. On the eastbound journey, with loads of around 300 tons, it was not difficult to make up substantial amounts of lost time. 4-4-0 *Celtic* for example, in its non-superheated condition, by running from Mullingar to Broadstone in 69 minutes recovered seven minutes of a late start, though this did not demand a higher average speed than 47.7mph over the generally favourable 37 miles from Killucan to Blanchardstown.

Not a great deal can be deduced from a comparison of the leading dimensions of the main line 4-4-0s on the four railways making extensive use of them, as in the table on page 22.

It was only on the Great Northern that the express locomotives were called upon to perform work anything approaching current English or Scottish standards, and there the Glover 174 Class, superheated, with 19in by 26in cylinders did much excellent work. On the GS&WR the one and only Maunsell superheater 4-4-0, No 341 *Sir William Goulding*, had no chance to prove itself because it was no sooner in traffic than its designer departed to become Chief Mechanical Engineer of the South Eastern & Chatham Railway. His successor, E. A. Watson, had altogether bigger ideas, and No 341 remained an isolated example. In nominal tractive effort it was slightly more powerful than the big Glover 4-4-0s on the Great Northern, but I have never seen details of any of the work the GS&WR locomotives performed. Because of their smaller coupled wheels, 6ft 3in diameter, Morton's superheated rebuilds of the Celtic Class on the MGWR, with cylinders enlarged to 19in diameter, were the most powerful 4-4-0s in Southern Ireland.

Watson received authority to build the first of his four-cylinder 4-6-0 express locomotives, No 400, soon after taking office, on Maunsell's move to England in 1913, and work was

IRISH 4-4-0s OF 1920

Railway Class Engineer	GN 131 Clifford	GN 72 Glover	GN 170 Glover	DSE 55 Miller	MGW Celtic Morton	NCC 70 Malcolm	GS&WR 321 Coey	GS&WR 341 Maunsell
Cylinders: diameter, in stroke, in	$18\frac{1}{2}$ 26	17 24	19 26	18 26	19 26	19 24	$18\frac{1}{2}$ 26	20 26
Coupled wheel: diameter, ft in	6–7	6–7	6–7	6–1	6–3	6–0	6–7	6–7
Total heating surface: sq ft	1361	1255	1366*	1094	1193*	1261*	1511	1856*
Grate area: sq ft	20	16.6	22.9	18.5	20	18	23	24.9
Boiler pressure: lb/sq in	175	175	175	160	175	170	160	160

*including superheater

actually started before the outbreak of war in August 1914. But because of war conditions, of the need to undertake war production at Inchicore, and not least the dislocation caused by the Sinn Fein rising at Easter 1916, it was not until late in the latter year that the locomotive was completed. Although fairly complete dimensional details were then published in *The Railway Magazine*, together with a frontispiece plate in full colour, little was known of the workings of this large and impressive looking machine until after the war, when news that further examples of the design were to be built suggested that the prototype had proved successful. In view of Watson's previous appointment as Assistant Locomotive Works Manager at Swindon, following his earlier experience in America, the many points of similarity in the layout of the machinery to that of the Great Western Star Class 4-6-0s seemed not without significance. Nevertheless the moderate scheduled speeds on the GS&WR and the infrequency with which loads of the principal expresses rose above 300 tons, there were some who questioned whether so large a locomotive was really necessary.

There was an interesting point in the arrangements by which the mail train locomotives worked through from Queenstown to Dublin. With loads not generally exceeding 300 tons and locomotives of such tractive power as No 400, the severe incline beginning at the platform end at Cork (Glanmire) could be climbed without assistance. The 12-mile run up from Queenstown would give an opportunity 'warm-up' and avoid the disadvantage of starting 'cold' up such a fearsome incline. At the other end of the line the start out of Dublin though distinctly adverse, was not nearly such a killer as that out of Cork. There was clearly a case for a powerful locomotive to eliminate double-heading, except in circumstances of exceptional loading. All the same, in view of Watson's evident predilection for Swindon ideas, it is perhaps mildly surprising that he based the machinery of his big Irish 4-6-0 on the Star, rather than the Saint. The former, with its nicely balanced four-cylinder layout and Walschaerts valve gear was ideal for long non-stop runs at evenly high speed, which the GS&WR did not have; the Swindon setting of the Stephenson link motion on the Saints, with negative lead in full gear, gave those locomotives a tremendous 'punch' at low speeds, and made them vastly better than the

Stars in slogging their way up very steep gradients. On the steep banks of the West-to-North route via Pontypool Road and Hereford they were better even than a Castle on the worst inclines. A valve-setting like that would have been ideal from Cork up through the tunnel towards Blarney.

After World War I, with the situation in Ireland becoming increasingly unsettled, it was something of a surprise to learn that no fewer than nine more of these locomotives were to be built, three at Inchicore and six by Armstrong Whitworth & Co at Newcastle. This latter order may have been at the suggestion of the Government to provide work at a factory that until recently had been heavily involved in wartime production, but where orders had by then become few and far between. What was a little surprising was that three of the Armstrong Whitworth locomotives were to use saturated steam, and a boiler pressure of 225lb/sq in instead of 175lb/sq in. The further history of these ill-starred locomotives is told in a later chapter. The only other new design introduced in Ireland in the immediate post-war era was on the Belfast & County Down, where J. L. Crosthwait put the first of his handsome 4-6-4 tanks on the road late in 1920. Like the locomotives of the same wheel arrangement introduced on the Furness Railway in 1921, they were not superheated, and the argument for this omission may well have been the same as that expressed to me in Barrow on one occasion, by E. Sharples, 'We can't afford superheaters on our short runs'.

CHAPTER 2

Irish Locomotive Men

The title of this chapter could well be regarded as something of a misnomer, seeing that in 1920 the locomotive engineers of the three largest railways in Ireland were Englishmen, who had held relatively senior appointments in England before crossing the water, namely G. T. Glover of the Great Northern, W. H. Morton of the MGWR and E. A. Watson, of the GS&WR. But in years of service Malcolm of the Northern Counties Committee section of the Midland Railway was by far the *most* senior, because he had been appointed Locomotive Superintendent of the Belfast & Northern Counties Railway as long previously as 1875, when he himself was no more than 22 years of age. In this he narrowly missed equalling the record of Daniel Gooch who became Locomotive Superintendent of the Great Western at 21. The retirement of another locomotive superintendent of very long service took place at the end of the war: R. G. Miller, of the Belfast & County Down, who had held office since 1880. He also had come from England, having been trained at Crewe, and subsequently seen service on that subsidiary of the LNWR, the Dundalk, Newry & Greenore. He was succeeded on the Belfast & County Down by J. L. Crosthwait, who had been District Locomotive Superintendent of the GS&WR at Waterford.

With this mention of the largest of the Irish railways the personnel of Inchicore require some extended reference, because affairs in the decade preceeding this survey had a considerable influence on subsequent happenings. In the early years of the present century when the British railways were making great efforts to encourage holiday visits to Ireland, it is to be feared that many people, showing a deplorable lack of discernment were inclined to regard the country as one where, to quote one writer 'people were expected to say and do funny things, and to be generally a bit mad'.

In that era, however, one could have looked deeply and in vain for any such traits in the locomotive department of the GS&WR,

when with Robert Coey as Locomotive Superintendent and R. E. L. Maunsell as Works Manager at Inchicore the whole department was run with a smoothness equal to anything in the British Isles. There was a fine team spirit throughout, maintained by W. Joynt, the Chief Draughtsman, and H. W. Crosthwait, the Running Superintendent. The last-named was a brother of he who transferred from Waterford to the Belfast & County Down after the retirement of R. G. Miller there in 1919. But when Coey retired on account of ill-health in 1911 and Maunsell was appointed to succeed him, the directors brought in from Swindon as Works Manager a man who was to prove very much of a stormy petrel, E. A. Watson.

The status of Great Western locomotive practice was by that time soaring to Olympian heights, and acquiring a man who had been Assistant Manager of the locomotive works at Swindon was no doubt expected to be of great benefit to the GS&WR. That he had had his training with the American Locomotive Company, and served subsequently on so great a railroad as the Pennsylvania seemed an assurance that the best of British and American shop experience would be brought to Inchicore. One senses however that Maunsell himself was a little hesitant in appreciation of his Works Manager, and was heard to remark on one occasion, 'Mr Watson thinks all Swindon geese are swans'. That did not seem to deter Maunsell from some extensive recruiting of Great Western men when he had to build up a virtually new technical staff for the South Eastern & Chatham Railway, in 1914. But the moment Maunsell was gone, and Watson had got his job he began to turn Inchicore upside down. It had been the intention to build more of the new superheater 4-4-0s, of which No 341 *Sir William Goulding* had been the prototype, but although the frames were already cut and some work had been done Watson stopped all this, and set the drawing office on to a large four-cylinder 4-6-0. He did not seem to establish a very happy relationship with the staff, however, with Joynt in particular, and in due course Watson sacked him. Maunsell had held Joynt in such high regard that when he got to Ashford and found the design of the L Class 4-4-0 of the South Eastern & Chatham virtually complete he asked Joynt to vet the details of the valve setting, and made some modifications at his suggestion.

Many years afterwards, I used to meet H. W. Crosthwait at meetings of the Institution of Locomotive Engineers in London, and he told me many a tale – some I fancy slightly exaggerated – of the stormy days at Inchicore during the Watson regime. Early in 1919 J. R. Bazin, with more than 20 years' experience on the English Great Northern behind him, crossed the water to become Works Manager at Inchicore. In England he had locomotive running experience and a spell as Acting Carriage and Wagon Engineer under Gresley in the latter part of the war. Some new blood was certainly needed on the GS&WR because Watson was preparing a large programme of new locomotive construction.

It cannot be said, however, that the utilisation of locomotives was very intensive. At the end of the war 4-6-0 No 400, and the one Maunsell 4-4-0 No 341 were working the principal trains between Dublin and Cork between them, with each making no more than one single trip of $165\frac{1}{2}$ miles a day. To cover the four expresses in each direction would therefore need eight locomotives, and this was evidently in mind when Watson sought authority to acquire a further nine of the 400 class, providing for two in reserve or stopped for repairs. Allowing one day a week for boiler washout, the planned utilisation was no more than 1000 miles a week.

Watson did not stay at Inchicore to see the nine new 4-6-0s go into service, for towards the end of 1921 he resigned to take up the appointment of Engineer-in-chief and General Manager of Beyer Peacock & Company. By that time the political disturbances in Ireland were mounting to something akin to full-scale civil war, and railways became major objects for bands of Republican guerrillas. The Great Southern & Western main line suffered severely; indeed, in addition to many smaller incidents, involving damage to track and burning down of signalboxes, the Sinn Feiners succeeded in doing what the Nazi bombers failed to do at any time in Great Britain in the second world war, destroying a main line viaduct and causing a complete breach in the line – this was at Mallow. Apart from this the damage elsewhere between Dublin and Cork was at one time so extensive that the 4-6-0 locomotives were withdrawn from service. As from November 1921 J. R. Bazin was appointed Chief Mechanical Engineer, but his predecessor did not last long at Beyer Peacock.

His health was failing and he died in 1922. With the formation of the London Midland & Scottish Railway in January 1923 R. H. Whitelegg of the Glasgow & South Western, victim for the second time of a take-over, left railway service for good, and assumed the job held so briefly by E. A. Watson, at Beyer Peacock.

Until he came to Inchicore in 1919 the new chief on the GS&WR had been continuously in the service of the Great Northern Railway in England since commencing his apprenticeship in 1897. On completion of this all his early experience had been in the running department, leading up to postings as Assistant District Locomotive Superintendent first at Colwick, and then from September 1906 at Peterborough. This latter, with its mixture of crack main line express passenger workings, and the very heavy mineral traffic, was generally considered the most important district on the Great Northern Railway. Then from May 1908 he went to Doncaster Plant as Assistant Works Manager, while in March 1916 he became Acting Carriage and Wagon Superintendent, reporting direct to Mr H. N. (later Sir Nigel) Gresley. It was an experience that could hardly have been more comprehensive. The only department in which he had not served since completing his apprenticeship was in the higher ranks of the Doncaster drawing office.

In Ireland, in the anxious times then prevailing, his earlier tasks were of little better than of 'making do, and mending', while taking the measure, as far as opportunity permitted, of the new 4-6-0s that were being delivered. An appraisal of the notable work he did is contained in a later chapter, particularly in respect of the increased responsibilities he had from 1925 onwards. As a measure of reconstruction after the end of the civil war a scheme of grouping of the railways of the Irish Free State was prepared, and duly approved by the Railway Tribunal of the State in November 1924. This, as a first step, involved the amalgamation of the Great Southern & Western, the Midland Great Western, and the Cork, Bandon & South Coast railways. Rather to the surprise of some British observers, who were familiar with the way appointments had gone at the time of the railway grouping in England and Scotland in 1923, Bazin secured the post of Chief Mechanical Engineer of the enlarged company, which came to include also the former Dublin & South Eastern Railway. So far as seniority as length of tenure of office was concerned, he was certainly second to W. H. Morton, who had been Chief Mechanical Engineer of the Midland Great Western since 1915. Although in relation to the mileage operated, and the number of locomotives, the MGW was a considerably smaller railway than the GS&W with 538 miles, against 1121, such considerations had not dominated the issue in Great Britain.

Furthermore, in Ireland the General Managership went to an ex-MGW man, M. F. Keogh who had succeeded to the post on the retirement of that most distinguished holder, Joseph Tatlow, in 1913. Be that as it may, Morton had to be content with the post of Deputy Chief Mechanical Engineer on the Great Southern Railway. As it turned out he seems to have been in close accord with Bazin's policies, and when eventually he succeeded him, it was to continue trying to make something worth while out of Watson's ill-starred 4-6-0s of the 400 Class. Before he moved to Ireland his career had been entirely with the celebrated railway contractors Kitson & Company of Leeds, which firm had already built quite a number of Irish locomotives. It would seem from the high distinction he achieved in his academic studies that he was more concerned with carriage and wagon rather than locomotive work, because as well as qualifying as honours man in engineering design at the Leeds School of Science and Technology, he became medallist (second place in the United Kingdom) in railway carriage and wagon construction. At Kitsons he became a leading draughtsman, and then Assistant Works Manager.

In 1900 Martin Atock, who for 28 years had been locomotive engineer of the Midland Great Western Railway, had reached retirement age. He was succeeded by his assistant Edward Cusack, a namesake of the Chairman and most probably a relative, and Thomas Atock, his eldest son, moved up to be assistant. But the MGW was not overflowing with mechanical engineering talent and W. H. Morton, from Kitson's was appointed Chief Draughtsman. Fifteen years later, having intermediately been appointed Works Manager at the small, but efficiently run locomotive works adjacent to the Broadstone terminus of the railway in Dublin, he succeeded Cusack in the office then titled Locomotive Superintendent. Until 1900 the company had not a single bogie locomotive. Apparently Martin Atock objected to paying royalties for use of the Adams bogie, and did not consider they were necessary in any case; Cusack had other ideas, and in 1902 put some very handsome 4-4-0s on the road, specially for the mail trains. It was he also who changed the locomotive livery from emerald green to royal blue.

These six replaced Atock's 2-4-0s of the Connemara Class on the mail trains, and the latter were in turn replaced by a new class of 4-4-0s with the same numbers and names, but smaller than the large 'mail' 4-4-0s of 1902. These 4-4-0s were the *third* class of six to bear the same numbers and names, the earliest being 2-4-0s built by the Avonside Engine Company, of Bristol, in 1869. Morton included locomotives of the third Connemara Class in his steps towards modernisation in 1916, and they like the larger Celtic Class were rebuilt with superheaters. One forms the conclusion that Morton must have been a singularly modest man. It is true that the Midland Great Western Railway was not exactly a speedway to attract those bent on recording exciting examples of locomotive performance, neither was there any appreciable publicity for its activities. Joseph Tatlow's celebrated work *Fifty Years of Railway Life*, makes no mention whatever of the locomotive department, but what could well be a mystery of later years came in the autumn of 1917.

Despite wartime conditions *The Railway Magazine* was continuing bravely with handsome colour plates, reproduced from oil paintings by the artist of the Locomotive Publishing Company, and each month there was a 'Pertinent Paragraph' commenting on the subject of the colour plate – until November. Then there was a characteristically handsome broadside picture of 4-4-0 No 6 *Kylemore*. But one searches the whole volume from cover to cover, in vain, for any reference to this locomotive, or for any dimensions. The presentation is in very striking contrast to another plate in that same volume, depicting one of Gresley's first 2-6-0s for the Great Northern, on which very full details are given below the picture. The caption to the MGW picture does not even acknowledge the design to Mr Morton. It shows that the gay royal blue livery had then been abandoned, and replaced by black, smartly lined-out in red, while the tender still carried the Company's coat of arms, flanked by the letters *MG* and *WR*. It took quite an amount of research to establish the origin of this locomotive.

In 1929 on the retirement of J. R. Bazin W. H. Morton was appointed Chief Mechanical Engineer of the Great Southern Railways. The economic situation was not such as to encourage any far reaching developments in locomotive practice, but in any case his tenure of office was relatively short. In 1932 he was chosen to succeed Mr C. E. Riley as General Manager of the Company — one of the very rare instances of a chief mechanical engineer receiving so high an honour. The only case in Great Britain that may be recalled is that of Sir John Aspinall, who prior to his return to England was Locomotive Superintendent of the Great Southern & Western Railway, and like W. H. Morton in his later days having his headquarters at Inchicore. As Chief Mechanical Engineer of the GSR Morton was succeeded by A. W. Harty, who since the commencement of his apprenticeship under H. A. Ivatt in 1894 had served entirely in the running department, first of the GS&WR in the Limerick and Waterford districts, and then on the major amalgamation in 1925 as Running Superintendent of the entire Great Southern system.

The Great Northern, becoming an international system after the establishment of the Irish Free State in 1922, was unaffected by the grouping in 1924–5. Following Charles Clifford's distinguished tenure of office at Dundalk the management looked to England for a successor, and in 1912 appointed G. T. Glover as Locomotive, Carriage and Wagon Superintendent. Although his most varied railway experience had been entirely on the North Eastern his technical training had been in London, at the Royal School of Mines, now a constituent of the Imperial College of Science and Technology. He began his practical training with Messrs James Simpson & Co, in London, afterwards transferring to Neilson & Co in Glasgow. From there in 1894 he joined the North Eastern Railway as a draughtsman in Gateshead Works. Between that date and his appointment at Dundalk in 1912 he was involved in almost every activity of the CME's department: testing of materials; boiler inspection; carriage and wagon works manager as early as 1901, and in 1903 engineer-in-charge of all electric carriage stock on the Tynemouth electrification. Next came the managership of Shildon Wagon Works followed by the Works Managership at

Gateshead Locomotive Works in 1909. Having served under such distinguished engineers as Wilson Wordsell, David Bain, on the carriage side, and Vincent Raven he then crossed the water to take up the appointment at Dundalk that he held for 21 years.

The Great Northern was then in excellent shape. From 1895 the dividend on the ordinary shares had remained constant at $6\frac{1}{2}$ percent for year after year, and even with the political troubles looming up it had not dropped below $5\frac{1}{8}$ per cent in 1912. It was the best in Ireland at the time. Dundalk Works was then responsible for maintaining 204 locomotives, 688 passenger train vehicles, 5811 goods wagons, and 295 service vehicles. The work force was approximately 700 men, excluding enginemen and running shed staff, and the total office staff was around 40. Glover set his standards immediately upon his arrival in Ireland, and they proved so adequate for the job that after the range of superheater 4-4-0 and 0-6-0s had been established, both in new main line and suburban tank locomotives and in rebuilding some older locomotives, no new designs were necessary until the early 1930s. From the outset it was evident that Glover had an eye for a handsome locomotive, and using the Schmidt superheater he avoided any exaggerated extensions of the smokebox.

Glover retired in 1933, not long after the very successful introduction of his three-cylinder compound 4-4-0s, which had made possible some welcome accelerations of the principal express train services between Dublin and Belfast. On his retirement the management made an unusual new appointment, which incidentally had a precedent on the Furness Railway before its absorption into the LMS. On the GNR(I) in 1929 G. B. Howden had been appointed Chief Engineer. As with Glover himself, 17 years earlier, the new chief had no previous experience of Irish railways, but had been throughout his early career on the North British Railway, and then in the Scottish Area of the LNER based mainly in Edinburgh. In Ireland he quickly proved himself a very able executive officer, and one of his early achievements was the notable reconstruction of the large viaduct over the River Boyne, at Drogheda, to permit the use of heavier locomotives. In 1933 the locomotive, carriage and wagon department was added to his responsibilities, as it had been to D. L. Rutherford, on the Furness Railway, after the retirement of Mr Pettigrew.

Combined responsibility for all engineering work had not been unusual in Ireland by that time, because on the Northern Counties Committee section of the LMS there had been the remarkable case of Mr Bowman Malcolm when the dual responsibility had come the reverse way. He had been Locomotive Engineer of the Belfast & Northern Counties Railway since 1876, having joined the railway as a pupil six years earlier. When the Midland Railway took-over in 1903 he not only retained his former position, but three years later was appointed Chief Engineer, and additionally Civil Engineer of the County Donegal Joint Committee Railways. He retired on 30 September 1922, just three months before the Midland Railway became part of the LMS, when he himself had spent 52 years in the service of the one railway, and no less than 46 years as a chief officer! He was succeeded in the dual office on the NCC by W. K. Wallace. Unlike Malcolm the new chief was primarily a 'civil' man, but he too had been on the NCC since his early training, and had gained wide experience under Mr Malcolm. He later crossed the Irish Sea and eventually became Chief Civil Engineer of the LMS.

Although almost from the start of his career on the BNCR Malcolm had built none but two-cylinder compound locomotives on the Worsdell-Von Borries system, when introducing superheating in 1914 he had changed to the more usual two-cylinder simple design for the two powerful U Class locomotives, put into service that year. Superficially, from such a detail as the shape of the running plate one could imagine some influence from the Midland Railway at Derby was creeping into his practice, but in the framing of the tenders, and above all in the use of inside Walschaerts valve gear the design was highly distinctive and individual. Only two locomotives of the new class were built in 1914, and another two were added just before Malcolm himself retired in 1922. When further new locomotives were required it was no more than natural that Wallace, as a civil engineer, would tend to lean upon Derby for guidance in locomotive practice, and from 1924 the NCC stud began to assume more and more a decidedly Midland look, enhanced by the adoption of 'Derby red' as the standard colour, instead of the 'invisible green' of the BNCR. When Wallace was appointed Chief Stores Superintendent of the LMS in 1930 he was succeeded by H. P. Stewart, Engineer and Locomotive Superintendent in Belfast. He in turn was followed by M. Patrick in 1933. Stewart had been chief assistant to Bowman Malcolm from 1915; he remained as chief *mechanical* assistant to Wallace, and was concerned with the important programme of locomotive modernisation put under way from 1924 onwards.

The individuality of the Dublin & South Eastern Railway largely disappeared after the grouping of 1924–5. Never one of the more prosperous of the Irish railways, its engineers were naturally handicapped by lack of capital to support anything in the way of an investment programme in modern motive power. Furthermore, there was no particular call for acceleration of service. Mr G. H. Wild, who succeeded the veteran R. Cronin as Locomotive Engineer had no superheated locomotives on the line until 1923, when two 2-6-0 freight locomotives with inside cylinders were built for the through freight services between Dublin and Wexford. In the Dublin area nearly all the passenger trains, both on the coastal route via Kingstown (Dun Laoghaire) and from Harcourt Street inland via Foxrock, were worked by tank engines as far as Bray. There, on the through trains for the south, 4-4-0 tender locomotives took over. Mr Wild had opportunity to do no more than put an improved version of the Cronin 4-4-2 tank on the road before the D&SER was absorbed into the Great Southern system in 1925. In the north on the Belfast & County Down J. L. Crosthwait remained in office as Locomotive Engineer for the whole of the period under review in this book; in fact he was still there in 1945, when negotiations were opened for the amalgamation and nationalisation of all transport in Ulster.

Plate 3(a) Ex-MGWR 2–4–0 No 657 (formerly No 33 *Arrow*) built at Broadstone 1898. Except for the cab, the locomotive is shown as originally built. It was later superheated and lasted until 1961. (*L&GRP*)
(b) Ex-MGWR 0–6–0 No 600 (formerly No 61 *Lynx*) of Atock's standard design introduced 1885, scrapped 1957. (*L&GRP*)
(c) Ex-MGWR: The last of Cusack's 128 Class of 4–4–0s of 1902 (originally No 124 *Mercuric*) as rebuilt and superheated by Morton. Withdrawn 1957. (*L&GRP*)

CHAPTER 3

Great Southern & Western: 1920–1924

Although the GS&WR system was in the thick of all the arson, violence, and guerrilla activity of the political troubles of the early 1920s, engineering was nevertheless at a high level of development at Inchicore, even though there was little scope for impressive performance out on the line for some years. Great interest centred round the workings of Watson's prototype four-cylinder 4-6-0 express locomotive No 400, and when it became known that authorisation had been given for construction of nine more, in 1920, it could generally have been assumed that No 400 had proved successful. This, however, had been very far from the case. A detailed examination of the design reveals some curious features from a man who came to Inchicore apparently so obsessed with the merits of contempory Great Western practice as to prove something of a nuisance to his chief, then R. E. L. Maunsell.

No 400 is supposed to have owed its inspiration entirely to the Churchward Stars, but it is surprising how little of fundamental Great Western practice was embodied in the Irish locomotive. It is true that the purely geometrical layout of the cylinders was the same, but there it finished. Watson used Walschaerts valve gear, but outside, with the valves of the inside cylinders actuated by rocking shafts. The boiler had a straight barrel, and the Schmidt superheater with a heating surface of 440 sq ft provided for a high degree of superheat, in total contrast to Swindon practice.

Plate 4(a) Ex-M&GW: Two of Morton's superheater 0–6–0s of 1921, Nos 634 and 630 (formerly Nos 40 and 93). The latter has the raised running plate of the later batch, built at Broadstone in 1924. (*L&GRP*)
(b) Ex-MGW: One of the Connemara Class 4–4–0s, as originally built (Broadstone 1910 No 25 *Ballynahinch*), scrapped in its superheated form in 1950. (*L&GRP*)
(c) GSR: One of the 'Woolworths' to R. E. L. Maunsell's SE&CR design, assembled at Broadstone 1926 from parts purchased from Woolwich Arsenal. (*L&GRP*)

The firebox itself was of conventional shape, without any of the special rounding and tapering that Churchward had been at such pains to develop, which had contributed so much to the moderate boiler maintenance charges, and which became the admiration of all on the LMS when Stanier took the design there from 1934 onwards. Above all, Watson used a boiler pressure of no more than 175lb/sq in, contrasting with the 225lb/sq in standard on the largest Swindon locomotive.

A steel casting supported the extended smokebox and in it were formed two steam passages, from each end of which were led bent solid-drawn steel steampipes to the inside and outside cylinders respectively. The seating for the blastpipe, and the exhaust steam passages were also formed in this casting. Exhaust from the outside cylinders was led by means of a breeches connection to the facing of the exhaust passage in the casting. The superheater was of the Schmidt type with 24 elements. A circulating system in connection with the locomotive blower provided for a jet of steam to be passed through the elements while the regulator was shut, at the same time keeping the cylinders hot and relieving back-pressure while running with steam off.

It is said that No 400 proved fast and powerful, but this can be considered in no more than a relative sense, because the nominal tractive effort at 85 percent boiler pressure was only 19,150lb against 27,800lb in a Great Western Star. It was not all that greater than that of a Glover superheater 4-4-0 on the Great Northern, which was 18,000lb as originally built, and 20,550lb when the boiler pressure was raised to 200lb/sq in. A commentator once remarked that No 400 approximated in size to a Star, but this can only have applied so far as physical size and weight, and not in any way towards haulage capacity. On the very moderate schedules of the day the No 400 took loads up to 360 tons, except on the heavily-graded sections at each end of the main line. From Dublin out to Clondalkin the maximum unpiloted load was 300 tons, and when piloted the assistant engine continued to Kildare. From Cork 240 tons was the maximum, and the up English Mail was nearly always piloted. With a load of 360 tons tare I have known the pilot taken right through to Ballybrophy with a third locomotive used to assist up the very steep initial bank out of Cork.

No 400 proved unlike its allegedly Great Western counterparts in two other ways. It was heavy on coal and water, and suffered from constructional defects at the front end. Like the Stars, the Irish locomotive had all the steam and exhaust pipes concealed with the smokebox and frames. They had many complicated bends and joints, and these led to fractures and leakages. No detailed logs of the running of this locomotive came across the water, but until 1920 when in service it worked opposite to the one-and-only Maunsell superheated 4-4-0 No 341 *Sir William Goulding,* which had a higher nominal tractive effort of 19,900lb at 85 percent working pressure.

When it was known that additional four-cylinder 4-6-0s were being built in 1920 there was surprise, not so much that the type was being multiplied, as that three of the six ordered from Armstrong Whitworth & Co, at Newcastle, were to use saturated steam at a pressure of 225lb/sq in. The cylinder dimensions remained the same at 14in diameter by 26in stroke. The nominal tractive effort was thereby increased to 24,620lb but it can have been little more than a 'nominal' figure. The details of the two varieties were:

	Superheater	*Saturated*
Boiler pressure, lb/sq in	175	225
Heating surface, sq ft		
tubes	1614	1870
firebox	158	158
superheater	366	—
Tractive effort, at		
85% pressure, lb	19150	24620

It will be noticed that in the new superheater locomotives of 1920–21 the heating surface of the superheater had been reduced from the original 440 sq ft of No 400. In the official description of the new locomotives published in *The Railway Magazine* of December 1923 there was a curious error, in which the boiler pressure of the saturated engines was quoted as 200lb/sq in, though the value of the tractive effort quoted could only have been attained with a pressure of 225lb/sq in. The six built by Armstrong Whitworth all had boiler plates $\frac{5}{8}$in thick compared to the $\frac{9}{16}$in of the Inchicore locomotives. This was evidently found necessary to deal with the higher boiler pressure of the saturated ones. There seems to have been some intention in 1923 of raising the pressure on the superheated locomotives to 200lb/sq in at some later time, and when the Inchicore boilers were renewed the plates were made $\frac{5}{8}$in thick.

When No 400 was put into traffic in 1916 it was provided with the then-standard Inchicore tender; it was perhaps significant of the reputation that the locomotives acquired for heavy coal and water consumption that on succeeding Watson as Chief Mechanical Engineer and taking responsibility for the placing of the new locomotives into traffic, Bazin designed for them a much larger tender. The relative proportions were:

GS&WR tender type	Old standard	401–409 class
Coal capacity	7 tons	7 tons
Water capacity	3345 gallons	4500 gallons
Wheelbase	12ft 4in	15ft 2in
Wheels, diameter	3ft 9in	3ft 9in
Weight in working order	37.3 tons	48 tons

An interesting feature was that all plate surfaces in contact with coal were galvanised. The axlebox covers had an auxiliary oiling hole with a swing lid, so that the oil pad in the bottom of the box could be replenished if necessary during the run without opening the main cover.

It was a most unpropitious time for the introduction of new locomotives. The damage to bridges and viaducts naturally restricted the use of machines with a maximum axle load of more than 18 tons. For while No 400 was more lightly built, and had a total locomotive weight of only 70 tons, the new ones with stronger frames turned the scale at 76 tons. After the destruction of the viaduct at Mallow the use of 4-6-0 locomotives between Dublin and Cork was abandoned altogether. On the through trains locomotives continued to be changed at Mallow for some considerable time, even after the new viaduct was opened in 1923. One of the Armstrong-built batch, No 405 hauled the Presidential train for the opening of the new viaduct. After the ceremony President Cosgrove with Sir William Goulding, Chairman of the GS&WR rode on the footplate of No 405, when it crossed the bridge slowly and severed the symbolic green, white, and orange tapes stretched across the track.

Some fast running was made with the presidential train on the return journey to Dublin. The load was no more than five bogie coaches, but the state to which the track had been reduced by guerrilla action was shown by the incidence of three speed reductions to 5mph, two to 10mph and three to 30mph in the total distance of 144½ miles. Intermediate stops accounted for 14½ minutes of the total journey time, leaving 155 minutes running. The opening section to Limerick Junction, 37½ miles, was one of the worst affected, taking 46 minutes start to stop. The remaining sections, 81½ miles to Newbridge, and 25¼ miles into Dublin were covered in 81 and 28 minutes respectively, in each case start to stop. There was plenty of fast running intermediately, including an average of 79½mph over the 9¼ miles between Maryborough and Portarlington.

Summary details of a run on the down day mail at the time when the 4-6-0s were working no further than Mallow shows a competent performance on the part of No 401, the first of the new Inchicore locomotives built in 1921. At the time the run was made the booked time for the distance of 144½ miles was 3 hours 40 minutes including a total of 14 minutes at the five stops: Kildare, Maryborough, Ballybrophy, Thurles, and Limerick Junction. The running time of 3 hours 26 minutes thus demanded an average speed of 42.1mph. On the occasion of this run however speed restrictions to 5mph were required at no less than *ten* places where bridges had been damaged, and there were four sections aggregating a distance of some 20 miles where hand flagging was necessary because of damage or destruction of signalboxes or telegraphic communication.

The train was a relatively heavy one of eleven bogie vehicles, weighing 363 tons tare. This was taken up the initial climb out of Kingsbridge, on 1 in 84, without a pilot, and the six sections run start to stop were covered as follows:

Section	Distance miles	Time min sec	Average speed mph
Dublin-Kildare	30.0	42 02	42.8
Kildare-Maryborough	20.9	23 52	52.5
Maryborough-Ballybrophy	15.7	22 25	42.1
Ballybrophy-Thurles	19.9	24 05	49.7
Thurles-Limerick Jcn	20.4	28 35	42.8
Limerick Jcn-Mallow	37.1	47 20	47.2

The total running time was thus 188 minutes 19 seconds, a gain of nearly 18 minutes on schedule, and an average running speed of 45.7mph. Without positive detail on the location of the numerous permanent way slacks and what was involved on the sections where hand signalling was in operation, it is not possible to estimate the effect of all these checks, but their cumulative effect was probably not less than a loss of 30 to 35 minutes in running, bringing the net average speed to around 55mph. When I rode the locomotive of the same train some years later in normal conditions the actual times over the six successive sections were 41 minutes 13 seconds; 23 minutes 30 seconds; 20 minutes 32 seconds; 23 minutes 08 seconds; 23 minutes 53 seconds and 44 minutes 25 seconds, slightly improving on schedule time throughout. Furthermore we took a pilot out of Dublin, for a load of 323 tons. On the earlier journey some very fast running was made south of Limerick Junction, with a speed of 80mph attained on the descent past Emly, and no less than 85mph near Kilmallock. This latter just preceeded a section of hand signalling, because Charleville Junction was one of the signalboxes destroyed in the Troubles.

The run with No 401 and a heavy load of 363 tons throughout represents a very high level of performance from the 400 Class locomotives, which they were not called upon to sustain — neither, one feels sure, would they have been capable of doing it. Photographs taken in the Cork district by Rex Murphy, with whom I enjoyed some diverting correspondence in years before the second world war, showed the 4-6-0s usually piloted on the ascent out of Cork, when the load was eight of the large corridor coaches. Quite apart from sheer pulling power they were troublesome locomotives, which spent far more time in the shops than should have been needed in the way of normal maintenance. An Irish friend once remarked to me that the only thing worth having about them was the boiler, and this seemed to find an echo in Bazin's first design of his own, and his subsequent practice. In 1924, just before the GS&WR was amalgamated with the other railways lying entirely within the Free State to form the Great Southern Railway, he designed a large new 4-6-0 locomotive on which only the boiler remained of Watson's practice; as he was appointed Chief Mechanical Engineer of the enlarged company, ably assisted with W. H.

Morton of the former Midland Great Western as his deputy, his policy towards the express passenger 4-6-0s of the old GS&WR continued.

The new locomotive, No 500, was a large mixed-traffic 4-6-0 with two cylinders only. It savoured of the design *dictum* so frequently stressed by another Inchicore chief of former days, R. E. L. Maunsell: 'make everything get-at-able'. In contrast to Watson's complicated 'innards' the new locomotive was a very simple machine with outside Walschaerts valve gear and nothing between the frames needing attention. It was only the second in what became a large series of powerful mixed-traffic 4-6-0s for railways in the British Isles, second only to Urie's H15 Class on the London & South Western. While Bazin on the GSWR had in mind the augmentation of power available for goods traffic, on which the six small-wheel inside-cylinder 4-6-0s of Robert Coey's design were becoming somewhat out of date, the existence of those severe gradients at each end of the Dublin–Cork main line suggested that a smaller-wheel version of the 4-6-0 express locomotive, and thus of greater nominal tractive effort, might reduce the need for piloting at both ends of the line, if a locomotive with smaller coupled wheels could make the necessary express speed on the fast running sections intermediately. Urie's 482 Class on the London & South Western had shown convincingly enough what could be done in the way of speed with no more than 6ft 0in coupled wheels, and while on the GS&WR Watson's 400 class could dash up to 80mph and more when making-up time, in the ordinary way the schedules of the English Mails between Dublin and Cork did not require maximum speeds much in excess of 70mph.

Bazin's 500 was as important as a prototype for future express passenger design policy as it was as a true mixed-traffic locomotive. The cylinders were $19\frac{1}{2}$in diameter by 28in stroke, but it was important that the 10in diameter piston valves had a long travel of $6\frac{3}{16}$in with large and direct port openings. The boiler was generally the same as that of the 400 Class, with $\frac{5}{8}$in thick plates, and the tube layout as eventually modified, having 168 small tubes instead of the original 173. The diameter of the superheater flues was $5\frac{1}{8}$in outside, as in the Armstrong-built 400s, but the elements were lengthened again to the size originally adopted on No 400, giving 440sq ft of heating surface.

The tender was a modified version of the large type used on the later locomotives of the 400 Class, carrying more coal and less water: eight tons against seven, and 3870 gallons against 4500. The boiler pressure was 180lb/sq in, which gave a nominal tractive effort of 23,780lb at 85 percent of the boiler pressure. In practice this latter proved a much more realistic guide to the capacity of the locomotive than the 24,620lb of Watson's non-superheated 400s. These lasted only a short time in their original condition, being fitted with superheaters at Inchicore and having boiler pressure reduced to the standard 175lb/sq in.

The prototype mixed-traffic 4-6-0 No 500 very quickly showed its paces not only in rapid hill climbing of the worst gradients, but in its greatly improved economy in coal and water consumption, and much reduced repair costs. The accompanying log of No 502 working the down Mail does not tell a great deal about locomotive capacity, except that it made a good start up the steep initial gradient out of Dublin. Maximum speeds at no time exceeded 65mph until the final descent towards Blarney, where 69mph was attained. It will be seen that schedule time was kept, or improved upon throughout — a schedule that with minor variations remained in force until 1939. Except in starting out of Dublin, where the gradients are successively 1 in 117, 89, 100 and 138 almost to Clondalkin, the locomotive had not been extended in any way. Unfortunately I cannot find any details of an unaided start northbound from Cork, where the gradient is 1 in 78, 64, and then 1 in 60 unbrokenly for two miles.

In view of the successful and economical performance of the 500 Class and the continuing troubles with the four-cylinder locomotives, Bazin decided on a very drastic and costly rebuild of No 402. Little except the boiler was left. The frames, cylinders, motion, and even the wheels were new. The locomotive had two cylinders 19½in diameter by 28in stroke as in No 500, and the same arrangement of the Walschaerts valve gear actuating 10in diameter piston valves with long travel. The boiler pressure was increased to 180lb/sq in. The nominal tractive effort as rebuilt was 20,600lb. It proved a very successful and economical machine, but the reconstruction was very expensive, and with world recession deepening and traffic dwindling the need for additional motive power of such capacity no longer arose. In fact the prototype No 400 was scrapped in 1929, while two of the

Load: 285 tons tare, 295 tons full
Locomotive: 2-cylinder 4–6–0 No 502

Distance Miles	Locations	Schedule minutes	Actual min sec	Speeds mph
0.0	DUBLIN(KINGSBRIDGE)	0	0 00	–
4.4	Clondalkin		9 30	43
10.0	Hazlehatch		16 20	61½
17.9	Sallins		24 50	54½
25.5	Newbridge		32 20	64½
27.7	*Curragh*		34 45	46½
30.0	KILDARE	42	38 20	–
6.6	Monasterevan		8 20	64½
–			p.w.s.	
11.7	PORTARLINGTON		14 05	
20.9	MARYBOROUGH	26	24 55	
8.5	Mountrath		12–05	62½
15.7	BALLYBROPHY	23	21 00	—
5.8	Lisduff		8 45	—
12.1	Templemore		15 05	65
19.9	THURLES	27	23 40	—
8.6	Goulds Cross		11 10	65/48½
12.9	*Grange*		21 20	—
20.4	LIMERICK JCN	26	25 30	
10.1	Knocklong		13 00	62½
22.3	Charleville		25 35	44
33.1	*Milepost 140*		38 10	42½/64
37.6	MALLOW	45	44 00	
9.9	Rathduff		17 00	36*
19.6	*Kilbarry*		26 40	69
20.8	CORK	29	28 35	

*Minimum on Mourne Abbey bank

Armstrong locomotives, Nos 404 and 408 followed in 1930 after a life of less than nine years. The history of the remaining six of the class after the retirement of Mr Bazin in 1929 is dealt with in a later chapter.

In following Bazin's developments on the big 4-6-0 mixed-traffic and passenger locomotives I have stepped a few years ahead of the life-span of the GS&WR and I must return to 1920 to mention something of the large stud of 4-4-0s. After all, there were nearly 100, including the McDonnell Kerry Class, and

Aspinall's celebrated 60 Class, built for the English mail trains in 1885. All of these latter were still in service in 1920, and used among other duties for piloting on main line expresses. But principal interest for the immediate future centred upon the Coey 4-4-0s of the 304 and 321 Classes, both of which were to be rebuilt in the 1920s to do much useful work on secondary duties. Before that an intermediate rebuild of an unusual kind had been applied to certain of the 321 Class, and until the multiplication of the 400 Class 4-6-0s began these rebuilds were taking a considerable share of the main line express work. When originally built in 1904 permanent way restrictions precluded any axle load greater than 16 tons, and the structural design of the locomotives had to be light in consequence. But with permissible axle loadings increased to 19 tons, rebuilding took the form of new and more massive frames.

This was a complete inversion of the normal conception of a locomotive rebuild, because the boiler, motion, bogie, and wheels were not altered, and the cylinders changed only by having a saddle extension added to support an extended smokebox of circular section. The new frames were $1\frac{1}{8}$in thick instead of 1in, and much deeper, and they increased the adhesion weight of the locomotive from 31 to 35 tons. The working pressure of the boiler was increased from 160lb/sq in to 170lb/sq in. The cylinders remained $18\frac{1}{2}$in diameter by 26in stroke; the coupled wheels remained the standard 6ft 7in for express locomotives on the GS&WR. The second and final rebuilding of these locomotives began in 1924 when No 321 was fitted with a new boiler having a Belpaire firebox and superheater, and a commodious canopied cab, similar to those on the later 4-6-0 express locomotives. The earlier Coey 4-4-0s of the 304 Class were also rebuilt to conform to this design, and together they formed a very useful medium-powered stud for secondary and main line piloting duties.

An interesting run with one of the 321 Class in its first rebuilt condition, non-superheated, was logged by the late Cecil J. Allen, conveying an unusual load for an unpiloted 4-4-0 on the GS&WR – nine corridor coaches, 286 tons tare and 300 tons full. With a clear road throughout no less than $8\frac{3}{4}$ minutes of a late start from Thurles was recovered. Details of the run are shown in the accompanying log.

GSWR THURLES-DUBLIN
Load: 9 coaches, 286 tons tare, 300 tons full
Locomotive: rebuilt non-superheated 4–4–0 No 332

Distance miles	Locations	Actual min	sec	Speeds mph
0.0	THURLES	0	00	—
7.8	Templemore	13	30	—
14.0	Lisduff	21	50	$43\frac{1}{2}$
19.9	BALLYBROPHY	28	45	—
21.5	*Milepost* $65\frac{1}{4}$	30	35	$43\frac{1}{2}$
27.0	Mountrath	36	25	69
32.5	*Milepost* $54\frac{1}{4}$	41	55	50
35.5	MARYBOROUGH	45	40	64/55
44.8	Portarlington	54	15	67
49.8	Monasterevan	59	00	67
56.5	KILDARE	67	15	—
4.5	Newbridge	7	50	—
12.0	Sallins	15	15	$64\frac{1}{2}$
16.9	Straffan	20	10	66
20.0	Hazlehatch	23	05	59
25.5	Clordalkin	28	45	68
28.5	Inchicore	31	30	—
30.0	DUBLIN (KINGSBRIDGE)	34	00	—

In the early stages the mounting of the slight ascents to Lisduff and to Milepost $65\frac{1}{4}$ with short lengths of 1 in 200 gradient was not heroic, but the locomotive was driven hard downhill, and gained $5\frac{3}{4}$ minutes on the easy schedule to Kildare. Good running followed on the generally favourable final stretch into Dublin. On another occasion, on the up English Mail, with a load of eleven coaches, at least 370 tons loaded, No 329 of the same class was piloted throughout by an Aspinall 4-4-0 of the 60 Class. Starting from Limerick Junction the two engines ran to Ballybrophy, $40\frac{1}{4}$ miles in 49 minutes, and made a smart run thence to Maryborough $15\frac{3}{4}$ miles in $18\frac{1}{2}$ minutes. On the succeeding non-stop run to Dublin they began well, passing Monasterevan, 14.3 miles in 16 minutes, but then were heavily checked by adverse signals in the approach to Kildare. But fast running followed with a maximum of no less than 75mph before Clondalkin, and the train ran to a signal stop at Inchicore platform, $49\frac{1}{2}$ miles, in $55\frac{1}{2}$ minutes, or 52 minutes net. Despite this stop, and checks at Kildare, the 51 miles from Maryborough were completed in $61\frac{1}{2}$ minutes, $1\frac{1}{2}$ minutes inside schedule.

47

CHAPTER 4

Midland Great Western: Most Irish of Railways

It was the late E. L. Ahrons who provided me with the subtitle for this chapter, and one senses that although he did not find a great deal to write about in the way of serious locomotive practice, he thoroughly enjoyed his visits to the line. But studying the articles from several other pens that have appeared in *The Locomotive* and *The Railway Magazine*, and not least the autobiography of its celebrated General Manager and Director, Joseph Tatlow, one gains the impression that it was a well-run, if rather leisurely railway; the successive holders of the title Locomotive Engineer certainly knew their business. In assessing the locomotive stock that came into the ownership of the Great Southern Railways in 1925, and bearing in mind that there had not been an absolutely new express passenger design since 1910, it is important to view the railway as a whole and its traffic requirements as it had existed before the merger of 1925. So far as the general philosophy of operation was concerned in the years after the end of the first world war, when Ireland had been rent by the bitter Civil War, there was by 1923–4 a desire on every hand to get back to normality, and to build up something of the traffic that had existed prior to 1914.

The Midland Great Western like most of the Irish railways was singularly free from competition, though serving districts that were thinly populated and yielding little staple traffic other than livestock and agricultural produce. Furthermore it had the difficult operating situation of three lengthy main lines. While the coast-to-coast route from Dublin to Galway, $126\frac{1}{2}$ miles, is the principal main line and marks the southern boundary of the system, there diverge to the north-west at Mullingar a branch $84\frac{1}{2}$ miles long to Sligo, and at Athlone another of $82\frac{3}{4}$ miles to Westport, at the head of Clew Bay. If one includes the 'light' continuation of this line to Achill Sound, and the eastward extension in Dublin itself from Liffey Junction to the terminus on the Northwall quayside there was a continuous line of 189 miles entirely under MGW ownership. Yet over this widespread system which with the various lesser branches made up a route mileage of 538, only 161¾ of which were double track, no more than 40 passenger locomotives passed into GSR ownership in 1925 and of these, believe it or not, 19 were 2-4-0s.

The goods traffic collected from such a widespread system, if not exactly heavy, required considerably more freight locomotives than passenger, even if only a few of them could be regarded as modern types. The company owned 51 of what were termed the 0-6-0 standard goods class, designed by Martin Atock. They were built between 1885 and 1895, and had 18in by 24in cylinders, 5ft 3in wheels, and a total heating surface of 1064 sq ft. The working pressure was 150lb/sq in. After the amalgamation quite a number were fitted with GSR standard boilers and superheated. By that time however they had lost the hallmark of Atock's locomotive practice, the highly distinctive turned-up cab roof. The purpose of this design is not entirely clear – it may have been to create an upward current of air to deflect the exhaust clear of the cab. With the leisurely schedules, even of those of the Limited Mail express trains, it was not often that the locomotives would be steaming hard, and when working under easy steam the exhaust might tend to drift down and obscure the look-out. Atock used it on all his locomotives, passenger and goods alike. It cannot however have been very beneficial when running tender-first.

All goods traffic in Dublin was dealt with at North Wall yard, on the banks of the River Liffey. It was convenient for the export trade in cattle and agricultural produce, and was of course more convenient for the commercial business of Dublin itself than the passenger station at Broadstone. The map shows the railway connections in the Dublin area. Traffic in the yard was extensive, and required the continuous use of five 0-6-0 side tank engines for shunting. These dated from 1881, had 18in by 24in cylinders, 4ft 6in coupled wheels, and originally boilers providing a total heating surface of 1065sq ft. They were numbered 100–103, and 105, and they became 614–618 in GSR stock. They were still at work in the North Wall yards 60 years after their first introduction, though like all other Midland Great

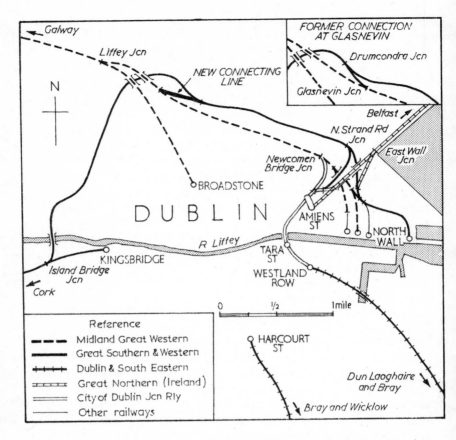

Western locomotives they had lost their picturesque names at the time of the amalgamation and the renumbering. Like many of the other MGW names their charm lay in their sheer inappropriateness! The four originals built at Broadstone Works in 1881–2, Nos 100–103 were named *Giantess, Giant, Pilot* and *Pioneer;* the fifth, added to the stock in 1890, was *Hercules!* They were sometimes referred to as the 'heavy' tanks, presumably to distinguish them from the little branch 0-6-0 tanks used on the branches constructed under the light railway arrangements to be referred to later; but as the North Wall yard engines weighed no more than 45 tons in working order they could hardly be called heavy in any other sense. In addition to shunting they were also used for rear-end banking of westbound goods trains up the steep ascent from the waterside to the junction with the main line from Broadstone terminus at Liffey Junction. The maximum load allowed to be taken up the bank without rear-end assistance was 15 wagons, and so the yard engines were kept pretty busy.

The increasing importance of the cattle traffic at the turn of the century led to the introduction of a 0-6-0 goods class of considerably enhanced power, with 18½in by 26in cylinders, and boilers interchangeable with Mr Cusack's new 4-4-0 passenger locomotives. Four of them were built at the time, numbered 143 to 146. Towards the end of the first world war W. H. Morton rebuilt them with superheaters and his own distinctive form of extended smokebox.

In 1921 Morton introduced what was claimed to be the first in Ireland expressly designed for mixed-traffic working. This was a superheated 0-6-0 with larger wheels than those on the Atock 'standard' goods, and on the Cusack locomotives of 1904. They had 19in by 26in cylinders, and 5ft 8in wheels, but were so designed as to have an axle load that would permit their use not only on all the main lines but all branches of the system, excluding those sections designated 'light'. With a boiler pressure of 175lb/sq in the nominal tractive effort at 85 percent boiler pressure was 20,500 lb, making them well suited to the working of fast livestock specials and regular express goods trains; they were also fitted with the automatic vacuum brake and steam heating, so that they could be used on passengert trains if necessary, including heavy excursion traffic that was worked on certain occasions. The boiler was of the same design as that used by Morton in superheating the Cusack 4-4-0s of the Connemara Class, to which reference is made later. The heating surfaces were: tubes 821sq ft, firebox 126sq ft, and superheater 210sq ft. The grate area was 17.3sq ft. The total weight of the locomotive in working order was 48 tons, and the larger tender carrying 7 tons of coal and 2800 gallons of water, 32 tons. There were eventually 23 of these useful machines which became Nos 623–645 in Great Southern Railways stock.

Mention earlier of the 'light' sections introduces the wild and remote branches out in the west, from Galway to Clifden, and from Westport to Achill Sound. These were among others built to aid the fishing industry and to open-up the country, as a means decided upon by the Government in 1890 to try and relieve the terrible hardship consequent upon the failure of the potato crop. The Treasury provided the capital free of interest for constructing the lines as 3ft 0in narrow gauge light railways, and the Midland Great Western found the extra capital for making the lines 5ft 3in gauge. Both branches were opened in sections, but they were completed by the early summer of 1895. In readiness for the light traffic expected on these new lines Atock designed a neat little 0-6-0 tank engine that could be used equally on passenger and goods service. They had 15in by 22in cylinders, 4ft 6in wheels, and an all-up weight of only 35 tons, with 4 tons of coal and 600 gallons of water. There were 12 of them, numbered originally from 106 to 117, and put into service between 1891 and 1893. Of these, Nos 109, 110 and 111 were built by Sharp, Stewart & Co and the remainder by Kitson. They became 551 to 562 in GSR stock. The line from Galway to Clifden was closed at the end of April 1935, that from Westport to Achill in October 1937, and with these closures the use for these little locomotives virtually ceased. However many of them were retained in service and moved to other parts of the Great Southern system.

Coming now to the main line passenger locomotives a total of 19 of the 2-4-0 type and 21 4-4-0s entered GSR stock in 1925. The former were all of the 13–24 and 27–34 series, built at Broadstone Works between 1889 and 1898. They had 17in by 24in cylinders, 5ft 8in coupled wheels, and boilers carrying a total heating surface of 1115sq ft. All were originally named, and Ahrons had some good fun in discussing the appropriateness or otherwise of many of the titles. Except for three, these names with their associated numbers all came from older 2-4-0s: Nos 13–24 from a series built by Neilson in 1873, and 30–34 built by Dübs in 1876. These earlier locomotives do not seem to have lasted long, but it was very different with the replacements built by Mr Atock, all except one of which passed into GSR stock, the majority being later fitted with superheaters. The non-survivor was No 20 *Speedy* damaged beyond repair in the Civil War. The three which were additional, and not replacements of older ones were those having names beginning with C, all built at Broadstone in 1897.

The complete class of twenty was as follows:

Plate 5(a) Tralee & Dingle: 2–6–0 tank engines Nos 1 & 2 (built in 1889) climbing the 1 in 39 gradient of the Glenagalt bank with a cattle train. (*W. A. Camwell*)

(b) Schull & Skibbereen: 4–4–0 tank No 4 (built R. Stephenson & Co 1888), shortly after leaving Skibbereen for Schull. (*W. A. Camwell*)

13	*Rapid*	23	*Sylph*
14	*Racer*	24	*Sprite*
15	*Rover*	27	*Clifden*
16	*Rob Roy*	28	*Clara*
17	*Reindeer*	29	*Clonsilla*
18	*Ranger*	30	*Active*
19	*Spencer*	31	*Alert*
20	*Speedy*	32	*Ariel*
21	*Swift*	33	*Arrow*
22	*Samson*	34	*Aurora*

Even the crack Limited Mails between Dublin and Galway could hardly be considered as fast express trains, even by Irish standards, at the turn of the century — or since for that matter — and with these 2-4-0s destined for the Mullingar–Sligo, and Athlone–Westport lines where the trains were a good deal slower still, there was a certain amount of latent humour in naming *Rapid, Racer, Speedy* and *Swift*. The LBSCR of Stroudley's day was, unconsciously perhaps, but much more to the point in naming one of its branch line tank engines *Crawley*. Like the Brighton engines of that same period the Midland Great Western locomotives of Atock's day had a smart and distinctive livery. All were painted a bright emerald green, including the underframes, with the background to the nameplates in vermilion. It seems strange however that the Locomotive Publishing Company, which so faithfully recorded Irish locomotive development in its monthly journal should not have included any coloured illustrations in its famous series of picture postcards by the artist whose real identity was concealed behind the pen-name F. Moore. In fact the only Irish subject in the entire collection was one of the Killarney Express of the GS&WR pulling out of Kingsbridge station, Dublin.

Plate 6(a) Great Northern: Rebuilt 4–4–0 No 107 at Enniskillen in 1932. (*L&GRP*)
(b) GNR(I) standard 0–6–0 as rebuilt by Glover to 1917 design, photographed in 1932. (*L&GRP*)
(c) Ex-Cork, Bandon & South Coast 4–6–0T No 463 at Ballineen on Cork–Bantry train (*W. A. Camwell*)

The third class of nineteenth century passenger locomotives that passed into GSR stock was one of six 4-4-0s that had begun life as 2-4-0s built by Beyer Peacock & Co in 1880. In 1900 the rebuilding of these as 4-4-0s had begun, though they kept their 16in by 22in cylinders. They had 5ft 8in coupled wheels and small boilers with a total heating surface of only 1053 sq ft. The weight of engine only was 41 tons, and 68 tons with their tenders. Originally they had Atock's characteristic upturned cab, but in the rebuilding a more conventional canopied erection was used. The names and numbers of these engines were:

2	*Jupiter*	26	*Britannia*
3	*Juno*	36	*Empress of Austria*
25	*Cyclops*	37	*Wolf Dog*

No 36, named after the beautiful Elizabeth of Wittelsbach, consort of the great Emperor Franz Josef, was to honour a lady who was a popular visitor to Ireland for her sporting activities. The origin of *Wolf Dog* was obscure. The animal is described as one of large breed, used to protect sheep against wolves, but today it would probably be recognised as the familiar Alsatian. The D Class locomotives as they were known were used on the Athlone–Westport–Achill line, and were still on that job when they passed into GSR ownership. Their names were then removed and they became Nos 530–535.

Mention of the Empress of Austria as a visitor to Midland Great Western territory in Ireland recalls the great popularity it enjoyed with sportsman generally, particularly fishermen. It was not only out in the wilds of Mayo or Connemara, but in many other parts of the line, and the company acknowledged the distinguished patronage it enjoyed by the building in 1902 of some of the finest passenger coaching stock that had so far been seen in Ireland. The basic make-up of the new Limited Mail was to include Post Office sorting van, two third class carriages, one second, one first, and the dining car, to which would be added through carriages from the packet stations at Dublin (North Wall) and Kingstown. These would be tri-composite coaches. The new coaches, with royal blue bodies and white upper panels, were most beautifully appointed, and such a train would of course have been far beyond the haulage capacity of Atock's mail engines, which were 2-4-0s, with 17in by 24in cylinders, and 6ft 3in coupled wheels.

Construction was authorised for six new express passenger 4-4-0s; the design specification included ability to haul a load of 308 tons at 60mph on the level, and to take a load of 281 tons up an incline of 1 in 100 at 30mph. These loads would be equivalent to eleven or ten of the new coaches, respectively. The basic load of the mail between Dublin Broadstone and Galway would be seven, and the additional vehicles would allow for the through carriages from Kingstown Pier and North Wall, and a through carriage from Dublin to Sligo (detached at Mullingar) and one for Westport, or Achill, detached at Athlone. This would reduce the load to about 250 tons for the 1 in 60 ascent to Woodlawn. Atock had retired in 1900, and it was the first task of his successor Edward Cusack to design new locomotives to meet this need. At other than the summer tourist season the loads would be much lighter, not amounting to more than four vehicles between Galway and Mullingar, and six from there to Dublin. Then it was customary to change locomotives at Athlone.

Cusack's first 4-4-0s were of a very simple straightforward design with 18in by 26in cylinders, 6ft 3in coupled wheels, and a total heating surface of 1363sq ft. The working pressure was 180lb/sq in. The locomotives had a neat and conventional outline, and would have been undistinguished in general appearance but for the adoption of a very handsome royal blue livery to match the bodies of the new corridor coaches used on the mail trains. This livery was finely portrayed in one of the lithograph colour plates in *The Railway Magazine* in October 1902. This livery had been tried out previously on one of the small 4-4-0s used on the Athlone–Westport line. As these were additional to the stock, not replacements, there were no previous numbers and names to be perpetuated, and the six were numbered and named thus:

124	*Mercuric*	127	*Titanic*
125	*Britannic*	128	*Majestic*
126	*Atlantic*	129	*Celtic*

I have not seen details of any running of these locomotives with a maximum load, but a run with the up Limited Mail in March 1909 shows that the demands upon the locomotives were very modest. *Britannic* was the engine from Galway, relieved at Athlone by *Mercuric*. The load was 128 tons tare to Mullingar, and 184 tons thence to Dublin. The following start to stop runs were made:

Stations	Distance miles	Time min sec	Average speed mph
Galway	—	—	—
Athenry	13.1	22 30	34.9
Attymon	6.2	11 48	31.5
Woodlawn	5.7	10 00	34.2
Ballinasloe	9.8	13 10	44.4
Athlone	13.6	20 05	40.6
Mullingar	27.9	34 12	49.0
Dublin (Broadstone)	50.2	73 25	41.0

Down the steep 1 in 60 descent after Woodlawn a maximum speed of 65mph was attained, with six consecutive miles at $56\frac{1}{2}$, 60, $60\frac{1}{4}$, 65, $60\frac{3}{4}$ and $55\frac{1}{2}$mph. It is reported that speeds up to 72mph have been attained by these locomotives descending this particular bank. Although with a very light load, the generally uphill section from Athlone to Mullingar was very smartly run, following a prolonged station stop at the former. The schedule over this section was 40 minutes, and a late start of $5\frac{3}{4}$ minutes was converted into an arrival just over a minute early at Mullingar. The run began and ended exactly on time.

In 1903 King Edward VII and Queen Alexandra paid a visit to Ireland and the 'big three' of the Irish railways all prepared sumptuously-appointed royal trains for their use. The Midland Great Western share was originally to convey them from Dublin to Galway, whence the journey south to Kerry was to be made in the Royal Yacht. But the weather was so bad that it was decided to go instead by railway and the MGW train was used for this. The first of the new 4-4-0s, No 129 *Celtic* had been specially decorated to work the royal train from Dublin, and was used again for the first stage of the southward journey as far as Athenry. There the one time Waterford, Limerick & Western Railway, by then part of the GS&WR, was intersected and the continuation to Kenmare was made down that line, hauled by another gorgeously decorated 4-4-0, from the GS&WR. It is of interest that the royal train provided by the latter company for journeys entirely within its own system included no fewer than five 6-wheeled coaches in its formation. The MGW train was a magnificent affair, consisting of five of the latest blue-and-white vehicles of the Limited Mail stock, in addition to the royal saloon.

News that the beautiful little 2-4-0 Mail engines of Martin Atock's design were being renewed as 4-4-0s came in 1909, though really there cannot have been much left of the originals. Reference to these renewals may seem a little out of period for this book, but in view of the part the further rebuildings of these came to play in Irish locomotive history some notes on these earlier happenings are not inappropriate. Provided with new cylinders 18in by 26in, and a boiler pressure of 175lb/sq, in the rebuilds had a tractive effort almost equal to Cusack's Celtic Class 4-4-0s of 1902, though to keep the weight down they had a very small boiler, and a Belpaire firebox with a grate area of only 16sq ft. The total heating surface of 1090sq ft was little more than that of the 2-4-0s, which was 1065sq ft and the route availability covered almost the entire MGW system. The new machines, for such they virtually were, replaced the 2-4-0s Nos 7–12, and took the same names. The first to be dealt with was the resounding *Faugh a Ballagh* in 1909, and the work was completed in 1915. (A free translation of Faugh a Ballagh is "clear the road"). The six locomotives (building dates in parenthesis) were:

7	*Connemara* (1909)	10	*Faugh a Ballagh* (1909)
8	*St Patrick* (1913)	11	*Erin go Bragh* (1915)
9	*Emerald Isle* (1911)	12	*Shamrock* (1913)

Three additional new locomotives of the same class built in 1910–11 were: 4 *Ballynahinch*, 5 *Croagh Patrick*, and 6 *Kylemore*. They were neat and compact, and proving a useful addition to the stock for the long secondary line from Mullingar to Sligo. The increase in tractive effort over the previous locomotives would have been welcome in getting a load under way, though the schedules did not demand anything of a sustained effort that would tax the limited steaming capacity of the boiler. By the time they were introduced the blue livery, for locomotives and coaches had been abandoned, Broadstone Works having reverted to emerald green locomotives and brown carriages.

On taking-over the task of Locomotive Engineer following Cusack's retirement, W. H. Morton began a series of experiments with superheating, applied to both the Celtic and the Connemara 4-4-0s. The situation was aggrevated by war conditions. The MGW had obtained its locomotive coal from South Wales; the uncertainty of supply by sea and the high cost of fuel had made any means of economy desirable. The loading of the more important trains from Dublin also was showing an all-round increase and the usual five coaches and dining car of the Limited Mail was frequently augmented by many 6-wheelers. The 4-4-0 No 11 was built new with a superheater and retained the same size of boiler. No light tasks were involved in sustaining steam pressure with the relatively heavy loads of the wartime Limited Mail. Four runs in the generally favourable direction from Mullingar provide interesting comparisons between superheated and non-superheated Celtics and the superheated Connemara No 11. On the third and fourth runs the six-coach corridor set was augmented by seven six-wheelers. Scheduled time for the run of 50.2 miles was then 76 minutes, average speed 39.6mph.

The start from Mullingar is adverse only to the extent of a mile at 1 in 200, and after that the line is level or slightly falling until east of Clonsilla, where the steep concluding descent into Dublin begins. The fastest running was usually made between Kilcock and the approach to Leixlip, through which latter station there was a speed restriction to 20mph because of curves. The average speeds between Killucan and Enfield give a good impression of level running, namely 52.5, 54.0, 45.9 and 54mph on the four successive runs, while between Kilcock and Maynooth the averages were 59.3, 50.4, 56.0 and 53.0mph. The smaller 4-4-0 No 11 made as good a start from Mullingar as the superheated *Mercuric*, but its average between Killucan and Enfield shows the need to avoid over taxing the small boiler and grate. Even though the average speeds were not exactly heroic, loads of nearly 300 tons tare were heavy for such relatively small locomotives, and the tractive resistance of 6-wheeled coaches would be considerably greater than of bogie corridor stock of an equivalent deadweight.

After the trials of the superheated *Erin go Bragh*, Morton in 1917 tried a larger-boilered version on No 6 *Kylemore*, of which

EX-MGWR LOCOMOTIVES: 1925

New numbers	Type	Class
530–5	4–4–0	5ft 8in branch
536–44	4–4–0	Connemara rebuilt†
545–550	4–4–0	Celtic superheated
551–562	0–6–0T	Small branch line tanks
563–613	0–6–0	Old standard goods
614–618	0–6–0T	Shunting tanks
619–622	0–6–0	18-inch goods
623–645	0–6–0	Superheater mixed-traffic
646–649	0–6–0	B class goods
650–668	2–4–0	Branch passenger

†There were two varieties of this series, according to whether they were rebuilt with piston or slide valves. The slide valve group, GSR 536 Class were 536 to 539 (MGW Nos 12, 9, 4 and 5 in that order), and the 540 Class, with piston valves were MGW Nos 7, 8, 6, 10 and 11. An intermediate renumbering of 1924 is referred to later.

Run No		1	2	3	4
Locomotive:	No	129	128	11	124
	Name	Celtic	Majestic	Erin-go-Bragh	Mercuric
	Class	non-superheater	non-superheater	superheater	superheater
Load:	axles	40	38	47	47
	tons	245	250	290	290

Distance miles	Locations	Time min sec	Time min sec	Time min sec	Time min sec
0.0	MULLINGAR	0 00	0 00	0 00	0 00
8.4	Killucan	16 00	14 00	16 00	16 00
14.5	Hill of Down	22 00	20 30	23 00	22 10
19.8	Moy Valley	29 00	26 30	30 30	28 30
23.7	ENFIELD	33 30	31 00	36 00	33 00
29.3	Ferns Lock	41 00	38 00	44 00	39 30
31.1	Kilcock	43 00	40 00	47 00	41 30
35.3	Maynooth	47 15	45 00	51 30	46 15
39.0	Leixlip	52 30	50 00	57 00	50 45
41.3	Lucan (North)	56 00	54 00	60 30	54 00
43.1	Clonsilla	58 15	56 00	63 00	56 00
45.7	Blanchardstown	62 30	60 00	67 00	59 45
47.2	Ashtown	64 20	61 45	68 45	61 15
50.2	BROADSTONE	69 00	66 00	73 30	66 00
Average speed, mph Killucan-Ashtown		48.2	48.7	44.1	51.4

there was a beautiful colour plate in the F. Moore style in *The Railway Magazine*. This retained the 18in by 26in cylinders of the original, but the boiler was considerably larger, higher pitched, with a larger grate of 17.25sq ft. The total heating surface, including superheater was 1145sq ft and the tractive effort at 85 percent boiler pressure was 16,700lb. The Celtic Class locomotives rebuilt with superheaters had 19in cylinders, and a correspondingly higher tractive effort of 18,600lb, though the boilers were very little larger, with 1193sq ft of heating surface and 20sq ft of grate area. The colour plate of *Kylemore* showed the wartime livery of black, with red lining adopted on the MGWR. This locomotive was one of the three additional to the replacements of the 2-4-0s Nos 7 — 12, and which were built new at Broadstone, to the same dimensions as Cusack's 4-4-0s. Nos 7, 8, 10 and 11 were eventually rebuilt to correspond with No 6.

Summarising, the 139 locomotives of MGW ancestry that entered GSR stock in 1925 were as shown in the tables on p. 61.

CHAPTER 5

First Thoughts on the Narrow Gauge: Into the Deep South and West

The sight of one of those dainty little Ivatt 4-4-2 tanks in the locomotive yard at Cork, and the thought of its original workings on the long branch lines out to the west coast leads one naturally to those remote and strangely alluring railways in Ireland built under the provisions of the Light Railways Act of 1883, and while in Great Southern territory to three in particular: the Schull & Skibbereen; the Tralee & Dingle; and the West Clare. It was not that on any of them one would be likely to find any notably significant examples of steam locomotive practice or stirring feats of passenger train running. Of one of them Lynn Doyle in *The Spirit of Ireland* writes:

> A Society for the Prevention of Cruelty to Engines would never have obtained a conviction against this line. A friend and I ran almost alongside it for some miles, in a seven-year-old car, and if the train hadn't taken a mean advantage of us at level crossings we'd have beaten it hollow. Most of the Western Light railways were conducted with similar humanity.

He does not specify what kind of a car it was, or exactly when this mild race took place, because I know of several present-day enthusiasts who have followed trains on Irish narrow gauge railways, by car, and had such an advantage speed-wise as to have ample time to stop and photograph the same train many times on the one journey.

Now before we go any further, I have a confession to make: I have never been to see any of the narrow gauge railways in the Counties Clare, Cork and Kerry. It would be pointless to plead excuses. It is just that in the years between the wars, which is the period this book is all about, life was just too short! Nevertheless several of my closest friends in the railway enthusiast world whose interests in that sphere are not so diverse as my own, and which did not include professional commitments in the same sphere, have between them made those railways of that period more completely documented photographically and on cine-film than any in the world. It has not been difficult for me with my personal acquaintance with the narrow gauge railways of the Irish north and north-west to build up a mental image of what the West Clare, the Tralee & Dingle, and the Schull & Skibbereen were actually like in the flesh, as it were.

Even with vivid memories of the County Donegal, the Lough Swilly, and the various lines incorporated in the NCC section of the LMS, it is difficult to set down in cold print exactly what it was that constituted the positively magnetic attraction of those Irish narrow gauge lines, and why an article in *The Railway Magazine* entitled 'Round Roaring Water Bay', published in May 1940, made a chartered mechanical engineer then hell-bent on wartime production, look back rather wistfully and wonder if in the years gone by too much of his available time for extra-mural railway observation had not been spent on modern main line practice! But looking at the map of south-western Ireland and at the countless photographs of three lines which at their maximum extent totalled no more than 106 miles between them, one can well ponder, particularly in the economic climate of today, upon how such railways ever came to be constructed in such wild and remote country, so far from any vestiges of industrialism, and where the staff would be utterly out on a limb so far as maintenance of the equipment was concerned.

I took down from my own library shelves two books published about the turn of the century which between them give some clue to the background against which successive Light Railway Acts were hurried through Parliament at Westminster. Neither was in the least political. Both were descriptive travel books, the one illustrated by very many pencil and pen-and-ink drawings by that consummate artist of the day, Hugh Thompson, the other by no fewer than 79 colour plates showing in all its grandeur of scenery and climate not only the natural features of the country but also the life of the people, particularly in the more remote districts. Both books were evidently written and illustrated to delight, and perhaps indirectly to attract visitors to Ireland, but neither could avoid giving at least some impression of the poverty and destitution that then prevailed in the mountainous and lonely countryside of the north and west, even though it was borne cheerfully enough and not excluding simple hospitality offered to a passing stranger.

The situation could be traced back in part to the grievous days of the great potato famine, and the steady flow of emigration to America that it induced. Thompson's drawings illustrate vividly how primitive were the means of transport in the west and north, and in the prevailing sentiment that something must be done recourse was made to the construction of light narrow gauge railways, which could be built far more cheaply than anything coming within the jurisdiction and surveillance of the Board of Trade and which would, it was hoped, do something to open the country and foster trade in cattle and agricultural produce. Inevitably they would be remote, connecting for the most part with branch lines far from the ordinary business and tourist routes; even though their construction and running expenses would need to be subsidised, their equipment had necessarily be of the simplest and cheapest that would fulfil the needs of the modest traffic expected. It was of course this very characteristic, plus the magnificent country through which they made their ways, that attracted the enthusiasts who were venturesome enough to travel there in days before the motor car.

Most of the English enthusiasts who visited the Irish narrow gauge lines that came to be incorporated in the Great Southern systems and wrote of their experiences tended to assume that the locomotives were a pretty shaky lot, in none too good a state of repair, and often driven in a somewhat slap-happy fashion. But this was rather in the style of the commonly-held impression of Ireland as a whole – an impression far removed from actuality. It is certainly true that in 1925, when the narrow gauge lines of the south and west were incorporated in the Great Southern, the majority of the locomotives were fairly old, and had been maintained locally when finances of the various independent lines had been sustained on no more than a shoestring basis. One needs to look back to the ancestry of the many different classes of locomotive running in 1925 to realise they were sound enough at the start of their careers, whatever may have been thought of them when they began to go to Inchicore Works for repair.

Just to name their builders and to see photographs of them when they were new or nearly new is to realise that they were first-class little jobs: the Hunslet Engine Company, Dübs & Co, Kerr Stuart and Nasmyth Wilson – all had reputations that were second-to-none. Hunslet, of course, specialised in tank engines in its early days, not to mention those three extraordinary freaks on the Listowel & Ballybunion Railway. The firm supplied more locomotives to the West of Ireland than any other manufacturer. The conditions in which the locomotives had to work did not improve with the years, although their weekly mileages became progressively smaller. All the routes concerned included some very steep gradients, and although the efforts required in climbing these were transitorily severe, the alternatives of hard and easy going were rough on boiler maintenance, especially when it came to be called for no more frequently than once a week! The Schull & Skibbereen, for example, had opened for business in 1886 with three tiny 0-4-0 locomotives required to take a trailing load of 30 tons up a gradient of 1 in 30; this they failed to do, and within a month of the first opening working was completely suspended. These locomotives I may interject were not of Hunslet make, but came from a firm that subsequently became very distinguished in the field of electric traction.

So, now, to a look at the narrow gauge stock and its working just prior to the take-over, by the Great Southern in 1925. One would imagine that the locomotive department of the GSR from its headquarters at Inchicore would have had some rather mixed feelings about taking under its wing such an assorted collection of narrow gauge designs, many of which could almost be classed as antiques, all suffering from lack of maintenance during the war years and the hazardous times of civil disturbance that followed.

The West Clare was the largest, and what could well be called the most unlikely of these railways. Its main line from Ennis to Kilrush was clearly never intended to provide direct communication between these two towns, the only ones of even moderate size in the whole county, with populations of less than 6000 and 4000 people. By road the distance between them is a little under 30 miles; but the narrow gauge railway made off westwards to the Atlantic coast at Lahinch, and then followed the coast on steep and sharply alternating gradients eventually to reach Kilrush, on the Shannon estuary, a distance of 47 miles from Ennis. The journey by train took about three hours. Just before the second world war the schedule time was $2\frac{3}{4}$ hours, but the West Clare was not the most notable of timekeepers!

With the branch line from Moyasta Junction, four miles from Kilrush, which ran out to the seaside resort of Kilkee, the total route mileage, all on single track, was 53. Before the 1925 takeover there were 11 locomotives, some of which dated back to 1892. These were built by Dübs & Co, to replace some rather feeble little 0-6-0 tank engines supplied by the Stafford firm of W. G. Bagnall for the opening of the line in 1887, and which proved pretty well useless. The conditions of working particularly on the exposed coastal sections of the route were unusual and hazardous, because in addition to the sharp gradients, up to 1 in 50 in places, the line is subjected to heavy gales off the Atlantic, and there was danger of vehicles being blown over. Coaching stock had naturally been built very lightly to minimise the tractive resistance imposed upon the locomotives, but it was found necessary to ballast these against the effects of gales by putting heavy concrete blocks under the seats. These, plus the sharp gradients and the side winds tended to overpower the original locomotives completely. After struggling for four years against delays, breakdown, and mounting ridicule the company obtained a 'Locomotive superintendent', from the staff of the Midland Great Western Railway, G. Hopkins by name, and he designed a class of locomotive that proved suitable for the job. These were the Dübs-built locomotives of 1892, all of which were still in service in 1920. With them the West Clare had joined in the practice that was almost universal in the south of Ireland at the time, of naming all locomotives, passenger, goods and shunting alike.

Hopkins having studied the prevailing conditions on the line specified the 0-6-2 type of tank engine, but unusual in that all the wheels were of the same size. He apparently had the idea that by doing this he could increase the tractive effort of the locomotive if found necessary by reducing the diameter of *all* the wheels. The position of the axle bearing could remain unchanged, and in fact he did reduce the diameter from 4ft 0in to 3ft 6in later. The three locomotives were named 5 *Slieve Callan*, 6 *Saint Senan*, 7 *Lady Inchiquin*. Dimensional details of these are shown in the table relating to all the locomotives of the West Clare Railway. Although these 0-6-2 tanks proved satisfactory from the traffic

WEST CLARE RAILWAY – 1922

No	Name	Date built	Builder	Type	Cylinders dia×stroke	Coupled wheels ft in	Boiler pressure lb/sq in	Total weight tons
1	Kilrush	1912	Hunslet	4-6-0T	15×20	3 9	160	40
2	Ennis	1900	T. Green & Son	2-6-2T	15×20	3 6	150	36.9
3	Ennistymon	1922	Hunslet	4-6-0T	15×20	3 9	160	39.1
4	Liscannor†	1901	T. Green & Son	4-6-0T	15×20	3 6	150	36.9
5	Slieve Callan	1892	Dübs & Co	0-6-2T	15×20	3 6	150	35.6
6	Saint Senan	1892	Dübs & Co	0-6-2T	15×20	3 6	150	35.6
7	Malbay	1922	Hunslet	4-6-0T	15×20	3 9	160	39.1
8	Lisdoonvarna*	1894	Dübs & Co	2-6-2T	15×20	3 6	150	36.4
9	Fergus	1898	T. Green & Son	2-6-2T	15×20	3 6	150	36.9
10	Lahinch	1903	Kerr Stuart	4-6-0T	15×20	3 0	160	36
11	Kilkee	1909	Bagnall	4-6-0T	15×20	3 6	150	36

†Scrapped 1928   *Scrapped 1925

TRALEE & DINGLE RAILWAY – 1924

No	Date	Builder	Type	Cylinders in dia×stroke	Coupled wheels ft in	Boiler pressure lb/sq in	Total weight tons
1	1889	Hunslet	2-6-0T	13 ×18	3 0½	150	38
2	1889	Hunslet	2-6-0T	13 ×18	3 0½	150	38
3	1889	Hunslet	2-6-0T	13 ×18	3 0½	150	38
4	1903	Kerr Stuart	2-6-0T	13½×20	3 0	160	—
5	1892	Hunslet	2-6-2T	13½×18	3 0½	140	32
6	1898	Hunslet	2-6-0T	13 ×18	3 0½	150	38
7	1902	Kerr Stuart	2-6-0T	13½×20	3 0	160	—
8	1910	Hunslet	2-6-0T	13 ×18	3 0½	150	38

working viewpoint, one suspects that the relatively long fixed wheelbase may have proved rather tiresome on the curves, of which there were very many, because in his next design Hopkins used the 2-6-2 wheel arrangement with the leading and trailing wheels fitted with Webb's radial axle-boxes, reducing the fixed wheelbase from the 15ft 0in in the 0-6-2s to 9ft 3in. The first of these, No 8 *Lisdoonvarna*, was built by Dübs & Co in 1894 and the second, similar except for increased coal-carrying capacity, in 1898. This was No 9 *Fergus*, and with similar basic dimensions the nominal tractive effort was the same as that of the 0-6-0s, with 3ft 6in coupled wheels. Two of the original 0-6-0 tanks were replaced in 1900–1 by 2-6-2 tanks similar to No 9, and these received names No 2 *Ennis* and No 4 *Liscannor*.

In 1902 Mr Hopkins had resigned, and was succeeded by W. J. Carter, from the GSWR. Although carrying the same title of 'Locomotive Superintendent', with only nine locomotives to look after he cannot have been much more than a running foreman, and later locomotives were built to the specifications of William Barrington, consulting engineer to the company. He initiated a complete change in practice, going to the 4-6-0 tank type, with outside bearings to all wheels. Cylinder dimensions remained as previously, namely 15in by 20in, but later locomotives of the type built by various manufacturers between 1903 and 1922 had differences in coupled wheel diameters and boiler pressures. The complete stud, as finally existing in 1922 and taken into GSR ownership three years later is shown in the accompanying table. As indicated, Nos 4 and 8 were subsequently scrapped, and the nine remaining locomotives were more than adequate for the service of two trains a day in each direction, which was maintained up to and through the days of World War II. As in the case of all other constituents of the Great Southern Railways, broad and narrow gauge, the names were removed in 1925.

The fascination of narrow gauge railways in remote and mountainous districts became evident in the very first volume of *The Railway Magazine*; following descriptions of the Snowdon Mountain Railway and the world-famous Darjeeling Himalaya line, this famous journal was not a year old before it carried an article on the Tralee & Dingle Light Railway. In more recent times there were occasions on its main line of 32¾ miles when it seemed to belie completely the idea of a somnolent country railway, dawdling along between intervals of flower-picking by the passengers. The sight of a pair of its 2-6-0 tank engines blasting their way up the Glenagalt bank on a gradient of 1 in 35 with exhausts shooting vertically upwards and a maximum load of cattle wagons was an invitation to make the journey to Tralee and log the running on the little railway for subsequent comment in the columns of 'Locomotive Practice and Performance'. Unfortunately, as explained earlier, I never got that far personally, though many photographs taken by my friends bear eloquent testimony to kind of performance that was involved.

The most spectacular photographic effects were obtained in crossing the mountain chain that forms the spine of the Dingle peninsula, attaining a summit level of no less than 680ft. For much of the distance, including the easily-graded first 10 miles from Tralee out to Castlegregory Junction, the line is alongside the highway, affording ample opportunities for the motorists of the 1930s to follow and photograph the trains; this proximity was the cause of special regulations being applied to the locomotives when the line was first opened in 1891. The first five were required to have an additional front cab, and all the motion was ensconced behind shields that extended downwards from the running plate almost to rail level. But these restrictions were soon relaxed and the front cab and skirts were removed. The first three 2-6-0s built by Hunslet in 1889, and supplied to the contractor to help in the construction of the line, were not only still in existence at the time of the GSR take-over, but survived until after the *second* world war, when the only traffic that remained was a once-monthly cattle special from Dingle to Tralee. This ceased in 1953.

There had been a quaint little 0-4-2 tank engine, No 4, built in 1890 by Hunslet for the Castlegregory branch, six miles long and virtually level throughout. Like the 'main line' 2-6-0 tanks it was

Plate 7(a) Belfast & County Down: The splendid 4–4–2 tank design of R. G. Miller – No 20, built in 1909. (*L&GRP*)
(b) BCDR: One of the large 0–6–0 goods locomotives No 10, built in 1914, and used on heavy excursion trains to Newcastle. (*L&GRP*)
(c) BCDR: Crosthwait 4–6–4 tank No 24, built in 1920 for the heavy and fast suburban trains between Belfast and Bangor. (*H. C. Casserley*)

originally encased throughout, and gave the impression of an armoured train engine. It was a tiny thing with cylinders 11in by 18in, having a modest tractive effort of 7050lb. It had been scrapped as early as 1908. The principal workhorses of the line had always been the Hunslet 2-6-0 tanks, and they remained so to the end. Five out of the total of eight taken into GSR stock were of this design. The last one, No 8, was built in 1910, being of the same general dimensions as Nos 1–3, of 1889, except that it never had a front-cab and skirts. The other three locomotives comprised a Hunslet 2-6-2 tank and a couple of Kerr Stuart 2-6-0s, which latter do not have appeared to be so successful as the Hunslet. The basic dimensions of the eight locomotives are shown in the table on page 68.

The Kerr Stuart locomotives originally had cylinders only $12\frac{1}{2}$in diameter, and boilers carrying no more than 140lb/sq in pressure.

Until April 1939, when the line was closed to passenger traffic, there were two trains a day in each direction between Tralee and Dingle. There were booked stops at Castlegregory Junction, Annascaul and Lispole, but the trains stopped when required at all the ten additional stations. The overall time scheduled was 2 hours 35 minutes for the $32\frac{3}{4}$ miles between Tralee and Dingle, which it would seem would not leave too much time to spare if all thirteen stops were made on the journey. Furthermore, on the very severe mountain section, both uphill and down, speed was supposed to be limited to 6mph with trains making a stop at the summit before beginning the descent in each direction. All stock, passenger and goods alike, was fitted with the automatic vacuum brake, which was very necessary in view of the loads of livestock trains frequently worked. On the heavily-graded section over the Glenagalt summit the load for a single 2-6-0 tank was four bogie passenger coaches, or two coaches and four goods wagons on a mixed train. On a purely freight train the load was seven wagons.

Plate 8(a) NCC: The last of Bowman Malcolm's 'heavy compounds' to remain in original condition, No 63 *Queen Alexandra*, not converted to a simple 4–4–0 until 1936. (*L&GRP*)
(b) NCC 'light' compound 2–4–0 No 51, at Coleraine in 1936. (*O. S. Nock*)
(c) NCC: One of the Class A heavy compounds as rebuilt with the smaller standard superheater boiler, No 69 *Slieve Bane*. (*O. S. Nock*)

On the cattle specials, 13 heavily loaded covered wagons plus a brake van could make quite a train for two 2-6-0 tank engines.

Moving still further south into the extreme south-west of County Cork there was the Schull & Skibbereen Light Railway, 15 miles long and opened in 1886. In the light of today's economic circumstances this may have seemed an extraordinary enterprise, for while Skibbereen is no more than a small market town of about 2500 inhabitants, the little fishing port of Schull has no more than 400; the only place of any size on the line, Ballydehob, is of about the same population. How could such a scanty community support a light railway, even of no more than 15 miles? At the time the railway was projected, although the human population had greatly dwindled from what it had been before the grievous famine years, near Schull there were some copper and sulphur mine workings that it was hoped could be developed into a lucrative traffic. This was a hope born to die, and the railway was in trouble financially almost from the outset, and dependent upon County Council subsidies to keep it going.

The performance of the original locomotives, or perhaps I should say the lack of it (!), did not help. They were surely the queerest looking, and most ineffective that have ever run in these islands. With their history I am not concerned now, but only one of the three originals survived the first world war, albeit in a drastically rebuilt condition. They were 0-4-0s, with $9\frac{1}{2}$in by 16in cylinders, and weighed no more than 16 tons. Of this trio No 2 *Ida* was the last survivor, and it was scrapped by the GSR in 1926. The backbone of the working were three 4-4-0 tank engines, introduced successively in 1888, 1906 and 1914. They were named *Erin, Gabriel* and *Kent* respectively, the latter two after mountains, and replacing the 0-4-0s Nos 1 and 3, which were scrapped at the same time. All three of the 4-4-0s had 12in by 18in cylinders, but the last two, built by Peckett & Sons of Bristol, differed from the first in having outside bearings to the coupled wheels. These three 4-4-0 tanks held the fort until 1936, when No 1, the first of the Pecketts was scrapped. That left the Peckett No 3 and the veteran No 4, built by Nasmyth Wilson as long ago as 1898, until the line was closed to all traffic in 1944. And then it was no longer possible to travel by train round Roaringwater Bay.

In 1939 the service by mixed trains consisted of two a day in each direction, covering the 15 miles in 88 minutes eastbound and 87 minutes westbound, with six intermediate stops. The service was arranged so that it could be worked by one engine in steam with departures eastbound at 10.00am and 1.45pm from Schull, 12 noon and 3.45pm from Skibbereen. The turn-round time at each terminus was 32 minutes. The track ran beside the main road for much of the distance, involving gradients up to 1 in 30; it diverged from the road only where even steeper gradients or undesirably sharp curves would have been involved. Even though the lengths of 1 in 30 were quite short they were more than the original 0-4-0 tank engines could manage. Until 1925 repairs to locomotives were carried out in a small works at Skibbereen, but after that they were sent to Inchicore.

That extraordinary affair, the Listowel & Ballybunion Railway, survived just long enough to justify inclusion in this review. Efforts to get the railway included in the GSR take-over failed, and it was closed at the end of October 1924. The railway preservation movement had not then started, and such picturesque English narrow gauge railways as the Lynton & Barnstaple and the Leek & Manifold were allowed to disappear. What hope could there be for this outstanding curiosity that was 16 hours from Euston? Connections from the night Irish Mail did not bring a weary traveller into Listowel until 12.40pm on the following day, by the line from Limerick down to Tralee. One can well imagine what a source of interest and pilgrimage such a unique monorail system would have been in a more accessible locality in these days of steam railway preservation. I have referred to it as a monorail, though strictly speaking the trains ran on three rails, though two of them carried no weight. The design consisted of a single elevated rail carried on angle-iron trestles, about 3ft 6in high. These trestles were supported on steel sleepers, each about 3ft 0in long, and on each side of the trestle was a light guide rail. The only function of this latter was to keep the rolling stock in position on the top rail.

Locomotives and rolling stock were alike of duplex construction, and amusing tales are told of the efforts the staff were sometimes driven to in balancing the loading on each side of the central rail. A good story is told of an occasion when one cow had to be sent from Ballybunion to Listowel. To balance this two calves were put on to the opposite side. Then, for the return journey the two calves were sent back again, one on either side! The three locomotives were built by the Hunslet Engine Company, and all the essentials were duplicated on either side of the centre rail, except for manning. Each boiler had its own firebox, but the driving controls were on one side only, applying to both engines. The driver had not only to drive the complete unit, but also to fire on his side, whereas the fireman on his side had only to feed one firebox, and had a relatively light task. But the length of the line was only $9\frac{1}{4}$ miles, and the journey time 40 minutes.

CHAPTER 6

Great Northern: 1920–1930

During the latter part of the first world war Mr Glover had been on active service as Chief Mechanical Engineer of the railway workshops of the British Army in France, and thus responsible for maintenance of all the locomotives used by the Railway Operating Division. He also held the rank of Colonel in the Royal Engineers, and his relation to the celebrated Colonel Paget of the ROD was similar to that of a CME on a British railway to the Chief Operating Manager. Absent from Dundalk or not, his organisation worked efficiently enough, and at the end of the war the line seemed to be in better shape than many of its British counterparts. The policy of rebuilding older locomotives of both 4-4-0 and 0-6-0 types that Glover had initiated had gone forward steadily, and some of the running made between Dublin and Belfast in the years just after the war would put to shame much that was being done in England at that time. It is of course true that apart from political troubles, which perhaps affected the Great Northern less than railways in what became the Free State, the Irish lines had not taken the tremendous beating from war traffic experienced by those in Great Britain.

At the end of the war the locomotives designated 'modern' by headquarters at Dundalk included the reboilered, but non-superheater 17-in 4-4-0s, and the 5ft 9in superheater 4-4-0s of the 196 Class, used mainly on the hilly road between Portadown and Londonderry. On the main line express trains the larger Clifford non-superheater 4-4-0s of the Uranus and Neptune Classes were the second strings to Glover's own large superheater 4-4-0s which he introduced in 1913 soon after taking office. The Clifford locomotives had 18½in by 26in cylinders, with the Neptune Class of 1905 having larger boilers than the earlier batch. The large brass nameplates carried on the sides of the boilers had been removed when the very beautiful

GREAT NORTHERN RAILWAY – 4–4–0 LOCOMOTIVES

Class	19-inch superheated	17-inch rebuilt	Branch superheated	Clifford Apollo	Clifford Neptune
Cylinders, in	19×26	17×24	18×24	18½×26	18½×26
Coupled Wheels, ft in	6–7	6–7	5–9	6–7	6–7
Boiler pressure, lb/sq in	175	175	175	175	175
Heating surfaces, sq ft:					
Tubes	975	1154	757	1245	1397.96
Firebox	141	101	106	116.5	133.34
Superheater	250	—	193	—	—
Total	1366	1255	1056	1361.5	1531.30
Grate area, sq ft	22.9	16.6	18.3	20	22.14
Locomotive weight in working order, tons	52.1	43.5	44.3	46.15	49.5
Tender					
water, gallons	2500	2500	2500	2500	2500
coal, tons	4.0	4.0	4.0	3.0	3.0
weight loaded, tons	30.55	28	30.55	28.0	28.0

green livery gave place to black. They were all of a simple and straightforward design, and of the handsome proportions characteristic of all passenger locomotives in the United Kingdom at that time. The valve gear was of conventional Stephenson link motion type, with short valve travel, though with ample port openings all locomotives of the series were capable of high-speed running by the standards of that period.

Little had been known of Irish express train speeds prior to 1919. In his hundredth article on 'Locomotive Practice and Performance' in *The Railway Magazine* in October 1918 Cecil J. Allen admitted that he had not at that time had any experience of Irish running. Very soon after, however, certain correspondents 'filled him in', as the saying goes, and to such a degree as to stimulate interest and enthusiasm for performance, particularly on the Great Northern main line. Allen seems to have been rather carried away in his own enthusiasm for a new subject to write about; even recalling that train timings had become very much decelerated in Great Britain by the end of the war, one cannot subscribe to his view, expressed in January 1919, of

> really brilliant running being called for by such times as 38 minutes between Dublin and Drogheda, $31\frac{1}{2}$ miles; 63 minutes from Dublin to Dundalk, $54\frac{1}{4}$ miles, with an intermediate 20mph slack at Drogheda; 28 minutes between Drogheda and Dundalk, $22\frac{1}{2}$ miles; 43 minutes between Dundalk and Portadown, $33\frac{1}{4}$ miles, including the Mourne Mountains summit.

Having regard to what had been done in pre-war days by superheater 4-4-0s on the London & North Western and Great Central Railways these schedules did not seem particularly brilliant, especially in view of the relatively light loads carried by the faster of the Irish trains.

Once the rather excessive superlatives are cleared away, the locomotive work on the Great Northern in the early 1920s can be seen as essentially sound. Nevertheless in view of what the same locomotives were called upon to do in the 1930s with similarly loaded trains, as related in a subsequent chapter of this book, a sense of proportion needs to be exercised in assessing the merit of the work in immediately post-war years. I may only mention here that in the 1930s net times of 33 minutes from Dublin to Drogheda, and of 23 minutes from then onwards to Dundalk – in each case start to stop – were not uncommon. Recalling these stirring runs and my own experiences of some of them on the footplate is a pleasure to be reserved for a later chapter. For the present, the gradients must be borne in mind. I am not sure if there was ever a wartime limit on maximum speeds over this route, as was imposed so widely on English and Scottish main lines, but whether this was officially so or not runs logged as soon after the war as 1919 and 1920 include numerous instances of speeds up to and slightly exceeding 75mph.

Going north from Dublin the gradients are undulating, without any more severe than a modest gable at Milepost 16 approached on each side by short lengths no steeper than 1 in 150. But after crossing the spectacular viaduct over the River Boyne at Drogheda there is a toilsome ascent of four miles up to Kellystown signal box, followed by a racing descent of five miles at 1 in 197 to Dromin Junction. The really hard work begins after leaving Dundalk with the 10-mile climb through the western ranges of the Mourne Mountains, to a summit at Milepost $65\frac{1}{2}$. The gradients are however not steeper than 1 in 100 at any point. The descent to the north is more continuously steep, for $8\frac{3}{4}$ miles, made worse for southbound trains because of the stop at Goraghwood (near Milepost 72), and the need to restart on the gradient. The timings remained much the same over the ensuing years except that the southbound Limited Mail was accelerated to a sharp 40 minutes over the $33\frac{1}{4}$ miles from Portadown to Dundalk. No new locomotive types were introduced in the meantime, except that there was a consistent policy of modernising the older ones by the addition of superheating, while a start had been made in rebuilding the original Glover 4-4-0s of 1913 with boilers carrying an increased pressure of 200lb/sq in. This is not to be confused with the later rebuilding of these locomotives from 1938, when they were almost completely renewed with heavier frames and improved valve gear.

However, to revert to the 1920s, a glance at the railway map of Ireland is enough to show that the Great Northern had some lengthy subsidiary lines in addition to its international trunk route between Dublin and Belfast. On these subsidiaries there was roughly three times the passenger train mileage of that on the main line. On the latter there were five through trains a day in each direction, on which it was usual for locomotives to be changed at Dundalk. The enginemen's duties were then shared between Dublin, Dundalk and Belfast crews, and even after the establishment of the international frontier the Dundalk men continued to work to both Dublin and Belfast. It was usual to keep the Glover superheated 4-4-0s with 19in cylinders on the inter-city trains on the main line, but with only eight of them available there were often not enough of them to go around, and the older non-superheated locomotives with $18\frac{1}{2}$in cylinders were called upon to help out.

Then in addition to the workings on the principal main line there was the long and meandering route from Dundalk to Londonderry, 121 miles of it, via Clones, Enniskillen, Omagh and Strabane, with three through trains a day, taking $4\frac{1}{2}$ to five hours, stopping at all the 26 intermediate stations. The principal route to Londonderry, both from Belfast and Dublin, was via Portadown, which joins the line from Dundalk at Omagh. Via Portadown there were good connections with the Belfast/Dublin trains, and the morning service connecting with the down Limited Mail was very much an express, covering the $75\frac{1}{2}$ miles from Portadown to Londonderry in 110 minutes with stops only at Dungannon, Omagh, and Strabane. Including the fast trains connecting with the main line expresses there were five through trains daily, as well as locals that ran only between Portadown and Dungannon. Another service that involved a considerable locomotive mileage was that from Belfast via Armagh and Clones to Cavan, a run of $79\frac{3}{4}$ miles. There were four trains a day in each direction, taking about three hours on the journey. Another busy and popular run was that from Belfast down the main line as far as Goraghwood, and then diverging to Newry and Warrenpoint, at the head of Carlingford Lough. There were up to 12 trains a day making this 50-mile run, though some were curtailed on certain days in the week.

The mention of these various secondary services, involving considerable locomotive mileage and time is enough to show that the total of 75 4-4-0 locomotives owned by the Great Northern was kept pretty busy. There were of course main line locals to be worked in addition to the through expresses. At the end of the war the Great Northern had nine 2-4-0 passenger locomotives, though these were naturally retained only for the lightest of work. They were of the class built by Beyer Peacock & Co in 1880, having 16in by 22in cylinders, but they had since been rebuilt with 17in by 24in cylinders. One of those that survived until 1932 was No 86, which hauled the ill-fated excursion train in the terrible accident near Armagh in 1889, and which, in attempting to take 15 crowded four-wheeled coaches up the long 1 in 75 gradient towards Hamilton's Bawn, stalled near the summit. The ghastly sequel to the traffic inspector's folly of dividing the train while it stood on the gradient has often been told, and needs no repeating here. At the time of the accident No 86, although small even by the standards of the day, was one of the class running the main line expresses between Dublin and Belfast.

In the ten years now under review no new express passenger locomotives were added to the stock, but much progress was made with modernising the 4-4-0s of earlier days. Mr Glover and his chief draughtsman L. J. Watson – no relation to Watson of the GS&WR – certainly made a very neat and handsome job of these rebuildings of the Park 17-in 4-4-0s. One can think of so many instances when old locomotives have been rebuilt, admittedly to make good workmanlike traffic units, but in which a handsome style has not been considered, and the result has been something of a misfit; but beginning with Park's four 4-4-0s of 1892, Nos 72, 73, 82 and 83, a most attractive medium-powered locomotive was produced. These four locomotives originally bore the names *Daffodil*, *Primrose*, *Daisy* and *Narcissus*, but these were not restored when rebuilding took. place. Their nominal tractive power was substantially increased by raising the boiler pressure from 140lb/sq in to the new standard 175lb/sq in. The smaller-wheeled 4-4-0s also introduced in 1892, having 5ft 7in coupled wheels, and originally confined to the Dundalk–Londonderry section, were similarly reboilered. The cylinders in both classes remained the same at 17in by 24in. The larger 4-4-0s of Clifford's design were rebuilt into units very little inferior to Glover's own, retaining their original size of cylinders, $18\frac{1}{2}$ by 26in even though the cylinders themselves were new, and furnished with piston valves and improved valve setting.

For the suburban traffic of both Dublin and Belfast the Great Northern was not really well provided before Glover's assumption of office in 1912. There was a class of tiny 4-4-0 tank engines with 15in by 18in cylinders, designed by J. C. Park, and six small 2-4-2 tanks, with 16in by 22in cylinders. Glover with an eye undoubtedly to first cost, designed his first powerful 4-4-2 tank engines as non-superheated, following in this respect the practice of the neighbouring Belfast & County Down Railway, and of the Furness Railway in England. These were originally designed to deal with the heavy commuter traffic between Dublin, (Amiens St) and Howth, and with the longer-distance residential traffic between Dublin and Dundalk. The original five of this type, introduced in 1913, were followed in 1922, by a superheated version, virtually the same externally. In the meantime the suburban traffic, particularly between Dublin and Howth, had grown to proportions quite unforseen in 1913, especially in the way of day excursions business on Sundays, and the new locomotives of 1922 were followed by a further five, and by the fitting of superheaters to the original ones of 1913. The basic dimensions of the latter, and of the superheated versions were as follows:

GNR(I): 4–4–2 TANK LOCOMOTIVES

	Non-superheated	*Superheated*
Cylinders, dia × stroke, in	18 × 24	18 × 24
Coupled wheels, ft in	5 – 9	5 – 9
Steam pressure, lb/sq in	175	175
Heating surfaces, sq ft		
Tubes	986.12	757
Firebox	106	106
Superheater	—	193
Total	1092.12	1056
Grate area, sq ft	18.3	18.3
Weight in working order, tons	65.1	65.75

The superheated locomotives were built by Beyer Peacock and Co. Ltd.

The Great Northern Railway on its formation in 1876 from an amalgamation of four separate railways – the Dublin & Drogheda, the Irish North Western, the Dublin & Belfast Junction, and the Ulster Railway – had inherited a diversity of oddly assorted locomotive designs, which the subsequent work of J. C. Park and Charles Clifford had not entirely been able to regiment into something approaching standardisation. But

GNR (IRELAND): DUBLIN–DUNDALK

Run No 4–4–0 locomotive No		1 113	2 171	3 174	4 173
Load, tons – empty/full to Drogheda		213/230	226/240	288/305	213/230
to Dundalk		181/195	194/205	258/275	180/195
Distance miles	Locations	min sec	min sec	min sec	min sec
0.0	DUBLIN (AMIENS ST)	0 00	0 00	0 00	0 00
1.6	Clontarf	4 10	4 10	4 15	4 40
4.8	Howth Jcn	8 40	8 35	8 45	9 25
6.7	Portmarnock	10 40	10 35	10 45	11 35
9.0	Malahide	13 05	13 05	13 10	13 55
13.9	Rush & Lusk	18 00	18 20	18 25	19 05
16.0	Milepost 16	20 45	21 10	21 20	21 55
18.0	Skerries	22 50	23 20	23 30	24 10
21.7	Balbriggan	26 25	27 10	27 20	27 50
27.2	Laytown	31 40	32 30	32 40	32 55
31.7	DROGHEDA	36 55	37 30	38 05	38 10
37.2	Milepost 37¼	45 10	45 10	46 05	9 40
43.6	Dromin Jcn	51 30	51 15	52 10	15 45
47.2	Castlebellingham	54 40	54 20	55 00	19 10
52.0	Milepost 52	59 35	59 05	59 50	23 45
54.2	DUNDALK	63 05	62 15	63 30	26 45

GNR (IRELAND): DUNDALK–BELFAST

Run No		1	2	3	4
4–4–0 locomotive No		190	113	191	174
Load, tons, empty/full					
to Goraghwood		147/160	156/170	180/195	225/240
to Portadown		147/160	170/185	180/195	157/170
to Belfast		147/160	170/185	180/195	244/260
Distance	Locations	min sec	min sec	min sec	min sec
miles					
0.0	DUNDALK	0 00	0 00	0 00	0 00
3.8	Mount Pleasant	6 45	7 20	—	7 40
8.3	Adavoyle	14 35	16 00	14 05	16 10
11.3	Summit	18 20	20 55	—	20 20
15.1	Bessbrook	22 20	24 40	—	
17.7	GORAGHWOOD	25 20	27 35	23 50	26 40
5.1	Poyntzpass	6 25	6 45	—	—
10.1	Tanderagee	11 30	12 25	—	—
15.8	PORTADOWN	18 10	18 55	21 45	45 35
4.9	Lurgan	7 40	8 10	—	8 00
8.3	Milepost 96	11 40	12 35	—	11 50
17.3	Lisburn	20 25	22 05	21 40	20 35
22.5	Balmoral	25 10	27 05	—	25 50
24.9	BELFAST	28 40	30 20	28 55	29 40

GNR (IRELAND): BELFAST–DUNDALK

Run No		1	2	3	4
4–4–0 locomotive No		173	191	190	172
Load, tons, empty/full					
to Portadown		177/190	220/235	233/250	236/250
to Goraghwood		205/220	220/235	233/250	236/250
to Dundalk		205/220	191/205	166/180	187/200
Distance miles	Locations	min sec	min sec	min sec	min sec
0.0	BELFAST	0 00	0 00	0 00	0 00
2.4	Balmoral	—	5 20	5 05	5 20
7.6	Lisburn	12 05	11 55	12 00	12 35
16.6	Milepost 96	p.w.s.	20 50	21 50	23 25
23.9	Seacoe	—	27 25	28 35	30 55
24.9	PORTADOWN	30 52	29 05	30 05	32 30
5.7	Tanderagee	8 10	8 50	8 15	8 05
10.7	Poyntzpass	13 35	15 24	13 40	13 10
15.8	GORAGHWOOD	18 40	19 35	18 45	19 00
18.4	Bessbrook	—	22 50	21 50	5 40
22.2	Summit	29 15	28 30	27 30	13 20
25.2	Adavoyle	—	31 45	30 50	16 55
29.7	Mount Pleasant	—	35 35	—	
33.5	DUNDALK	40 45	39 10	40 30	24 50
	Schedule times, minutes	31	30	30	30
		43	40	40	20
					27

GNR (IRELAND): DUNDALK–DUBLIN

Run No			1		2		3		4	
4–4–0 locomotive No			113		114		172		170	
Load, tons, empty/full			205/230		220/235		250/265		250/265	
Distance miles	Locations		min	sec	min	sec	min	sec	min	sec
0.0	DUNDALK		0	00	0	00	0	00	0	00
7.0	Castlebellingham		10	55	10	10	10	35	10	40
10.6	Dromin Jcn		—		14	00	14	30	14	35
17.0	Milepost 37½		—		21	55	22	20	21	30
22.5	DROGHEDA		27	55	27	45	28	10	27	35
4.5	Laytown		7	05	6	35	6	35	7	15
10.0	Balbriggan		—		11	50	12	05	12	35
15.7	Milepost 16		—		18	05	18	35	18	55
22.7	Malahide		26	00	25	10	25	10	25	30
26.9	Howth Jcn		30	05	29	55	29	20	29	45
30.1	Clontarf		—		33	35	32	35	33	05
31.7	DUBLIN (AMIENS ST)		37	00	36	15	35	05	36	00
	Schedule times, minutes		28		27		27		27	
			38		37		37		37	

Glover by his own new designs and by his policy of rebuilding was by the early 1920s imposing a remarkable measure of reform. His large superheated 0-6-0 goods class with 19in by 26in cylinders had boilers interchangeable with the 170 Class express passenger locomotives, while his rebuilding of many earlier 0-6-0s provided them with boilers that were likewise interchangeable with those of 4-4-0s rebuilt from earlier designs. It will be seen also that the boilers of the new standard branch 4-4-0s with 5ft 9in coupled wheels, as shown in the table on page 78 are the same as those of the superheated version of the 4-4-2 tanks.

It is now appropriate to conclude this first survey with some actual reference to work on the line. Although this concerns almost entirely the main route between Dublin and Belfast, it was of course there that all the hardest and fastest running was needed. For ready reference I have prepared four tables dividing the route into the two sections north and south of Dundalk, where at the period under review it became customary for all the regular express passenger trains to change engines. This was not so just at the end of the war. The first table shows details of four runs from Dublin to Dundalk. The only serious hindrance was the severe speed restriction to 15mph through Drogheda, because immediately following it came the climb up to Milepost $37\frac{1}{4}$. On the first three runs, non-stop to Dundalk, the times were very similar as far as Laytown, despite the variation in loading. The non-superheated Clifford 4-4-0 actually made the fastest running over this first stage with a top speed of 66mph at Skerries after a minimum of 46mph at Milepost 16. The second run was probably hampered by a strong cross-wind and rain. Both trains slipped a coach at Drogheda, but afterwards the superheated No 171 made much the better running despite the adverse weather conditions.

Plate 9(a) County Donegal 2–6–4 tank No 17 *Glenties*, built by Nasmyth Wilson and Co in 1907. Renumbered 5 and renamed *Drumboe* in 1937. (*L&GRP*)
(b) Londonderry & Lough Swilly 4–6–2 tank No 7, built by Hudswell Clark & Co in 1901. (*L&GRP*)
(c) County Donegal Railway 2–6–4 tank No 16 *Donegal* on train at Strabane. This locomotive was renumbered 4 and renamed *Meenglas* in 1937. (*L&GRP*)

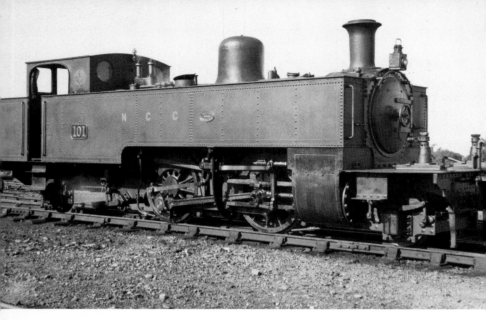

Plate 10(a) NCC: Bowman Malcolm two-cylinder compound 2–4–2 tank No 101, working on the Ballycastle line in 1936. (*L&GRP*)

(b) Londonderry & Lough Swilly 4–6–2 tank No 10 on a typical mixed train in 1927. (*L&GRP*)

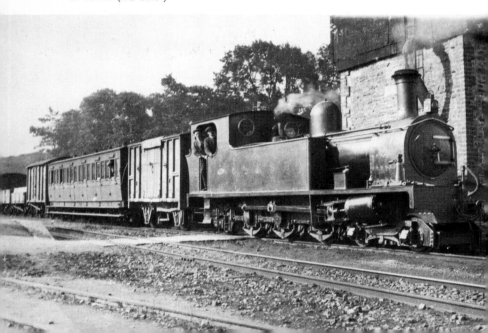

The driver of No 171, Micky O'Farrell, became something of a legend as English enthusiasts crossed the water and recorded running on the Great Northern. He had retired before my own travelling in Ireland began, but Cecil J. Allen and J. Macartney Robbins used to try and plan their journeys to coincide with his turns on the fast trains. On this run he accelerated from the Drogheda slack to 50mph up the 1 in 177 to Milepost $37\frac{1}{4}$, and then touched 74mph on the fast descent to Castlebellingham. The corresponding speeds by the non-superheated No 113 were 46mph and 75mph; both trains arrived in Dundalk ahead of the scheduled 64minutes. On the third journey with a much heavier train engine No 173 made almost identical times to those of No 171 to Laytown, but the passage through Drogheda was slow, and the heavier load took its toll up the subsequent bank, where speed did not rise above 43mph. At the summit No 173 was nearly a minute behind the other two locomotives, but with some fast downhill running Dundalk was reached just inside schedule time. On the last run No 173 attained $41\frac{1}{2}$mph up the bank from the restart at Drogheda, but with 27 minutes for the 22.5 miles to Dundalk had no need for undue haste afterwards.

The second table, showing the work northwards from Dundalk, is of interest as indicating the performance on the heavy ascent to the summit at Milepost $65\frac{1}{4}$; the loads were so relatively light as to provide no serious tax upon locomotive capacity. Unfortunately the recorder of run No 3, the fastest by far, took no detail other than the passing time at Adavoyle, and the subsequent maximum speed of 75mph before the stop at Goraghwood. The second fastest, that with No 190, involved speeds of $32\frac{1}{2}$mph on the 1 in 100 out of Dundalk, an increase to 38mph on the slightly easier length to Adavoyle, and 40mph over the summit. The non-superheated locomotive did comparatively poor work uphill, but the driver did his best to retrieve things by a speed of $77\frac{1}{2}$mph before Goraghwood. On the fourth run, non-stop to Portadown, the uphill speeds were inferior to those of runs 1 and 3, and one can never make much running on the favourably graded section north of Goraghwood, because of speed restrictions for curves at Poyntzpass and Scarva. Finally, the gradients up to Milepost 96 are nowhere steeper than 1 in 210 after which it is a downhill run from Lisburn into Belfast.

The third table gives details of four runs southbound from

Belfast to Dundalk. All drivers began easily on the rise out of the terminus, which ends at Lisburn, after which speed ranged round 60mph onwards to Milepost 96, with speeds up to a maximum of 75mph by Seagoe Box. On the fourth run the driver of No 172 evidently misjudged things to lose $2\frac{1}{2}$ minutes on schedule, though he made ample amends afterwards, doing well to reach Goraghwood in 19 minutes. On runs 2 and 3 the up Limited Mail slipped a coach for Warrenpoint, and No 190, which had got away from Portadown very smartly, fell back very gradually to a minimum of 36mph on the 1 in 100 gradient to the summit. No 191, which had fallen back somewhat from the start, sustained 38mph up the last stages of the climb, but was nevertheless, a minute behind the sister locomotive at the summit. But whereas No 190 was taken downhill so gently as to lose $\frac{1}{2}$ minute on booked time to Dundalk, No 191 came down like a thunderbolt, touching 80mph and gaining $\frac{3}{4}$ minute. In the last column No 172 attained 34mph on the climb from the restart at Goraghwood, and running smartly downhill, with a maximum of $71\frac{1}{2}$mph gained $2\frac{1}{4}$ minutes to Dundalk.

The last table, showing work from Dundalk into Dublin, is interesting as including examples of four different varieties of 4-4-0. The first, No 113, is a Clifford non-superheater; the second is of the same class but rebuilt and superheated, though retaining $18\frac{1}{2}$ diameter cylinders; the third is a standard Glover 19-in superheater 4-4-0; the last is a locomotive of the same class, but rebuilt with a boiler carrying 200lb/sq in pressure. From the tabulated details one cannot say that there were any significant differences to be discerned between the four locomotives, all of which lost small amounts of time to Drogheda, except the non-superheated No 113, on a slightly easier schedule, but had things well in hand onwards to Dublin. I can only say that these standards might be borne in mind for comparison with what the same locomotives were required to do in the later 1930s, when I personally recorded times of 18 minutes 33 seconds passing Milepost $37\frac{1}{4}$ from Dundalk, and of 29 minutes 37 seconds passing Clontarf from Drogheda, with No 173 and a 260-ton load. Detailed reference to such spirited work must be kept for a later chapter in this book.

CHAPTER 7

Belfast & County Down:
A Railway in Decline

At the time when this book opens the Belfast & County Down was one of the most prosperous railways in the whole of the British Isles. Twenty years later it seemed that little could save it from going into liquidation. True, it was no more than a minor railway, little more so than some of the one-time independent railways of South Wales, but all the movements towards grouping in the 1920s passed it by. The Great Southern was concerned with no railways that lay outside Eire, leaving out in the cold such lines as the County Donegal, and the Lough Swilly which had a small proportion of their mileage in Northern Ireland. The Great Northern had its own problems, as an inter-city, international trunk route. In other circumstances the LMS, as parent of the Northern Counties Committee lines, might have looked towards the 'County Down', with a view to scooping it into its empire. The sagatious local management of the NCC, only just on the opposite side of Lough Foyle, would have been well enough aware of the problems that were creeping up on the 'County Down', and were no doubt canny enough to advise their masters in far-away Euston to leave well alone. So the hapless 'County Down' remained independent, ungrouped, out on a limb, with its one-time prosperity visibly dissolving before its eyes.

The BCDR was in many ways a period-piece in the history of inland transport; its rapid decline after 1924 was no reflection upon the efficiency of its operation and management, but a sign of the rapidly-changing times. Had the environment offered the chance, there is little doubt that its far-sighted senior executives would have sought out and exploited new traffics to try and replace those that were dwindling, but in County Down those opportunities just did not exist. A study of the map alone can be revealing. It is perhaps an exaggeration to suggest that much of the county, although so near to Belfast, is as rural and remote as Connemara. The furthest extent of the line, Newcastle – 'where the Mountains of Mourne sweep down to the sea' – and only 38 miles from Belfast, is a tourist resort above all else, and there in 1898 the company had built the magnificent Slieve Donard hotel. Adjacent to excellent golf links it was hoped that it would eventually become an Irish counterpart – indeed a forerunner – of famous railway hotels at Gleneagles, Turnbery and Dornoch. At the time of its construction it was claimed to be the largest and finest in all Ireland.

The line to Newcastle came as something of an after-thought to the original project, which was to connect Belfast to the county town of Downpatrick, and was opened throughout in 1859. Downpatrick station was constructed as a terminus, a situation that left the railway with an inconvenience in operation that remained in perpetuity. The extension to Newcastle was made by a separate company, though worked by the Belfast & County Down from the outset. This line, $11\frac{1}{2}$ miles long, was opened in 1869. At first, trains for Newcastle had to reverse at Downpatrick, but in 1891 an avoiding line was authorised to enable trains to run direct to Newcastle without the need for this. This avoiding line over the bog land of the Quoile River estuary was constructed in the style of Chat Moss, on a thick layer of brushwood spread on the surface of this treacherous ground.

While the development of tourist attractions at Newcastle was one of the unfulfilled hopes of the Belfast & County Down Railway, the line to the south was not exactly built as an express route. As far as Comber, eight miles out, where the branch to Donaghadee went off, the gradients were not difficult, but on continuing there was a stiff ascent at 1 in 150 to Ballygowan and sharp undulations, mostly at 1 in 100, until Ballynahinch Junction was reached. The gradients reflected the way in which the line was engineered through this hilly country to minimise the cost of construction by avoiding large earthworks. The descent from Ballynahinch Junction to Crossgar is even worse, for three miles almost continuously at 1 in 100. The branch line from Comber to Donaghadee was another of the unfulfilled hopes of the Belfast and County Down Railway, because the grandiose project of making Donaghadee a packet station and establishing a Royal Mail service between there and Portpatrick in Wigtownshire came to nought. Donaghadee is only 22 miles from Belfast by rail, but the alignment of the track is hardly such as to permit such fast running of the boat trains as became customary in later years between Belfast and Larne by the NCC route.

The real money-spinner so far as the BNCR was concerned became the commuter run along the south shore of Belfast Lough to Bangor. It is only $12\frac{1}{4}$ miles long, but there are seven intermediate stations, and of the 50-odd trains that used to leave Belfast (Queens Quay) station daily some went no further than Holywood, $4\frac{1}{2}$ miles out, while some terminated at Craigavad. There were one or two non-stop trains that did the $12\frac{1}{4}$ mile journey in 20 minutes. Despite being so relatively small and local a railway it was very efficiently run. At the height of its passenger activity there were more than 170 trains in and out of Queens Quay station daily, and yet the company owned no more than 30 locomotives. The diagrams were most skilfully worked out to get the maximum utilisation out of every locomotive. Of the BNCR it could never be said that there were large numbers of locomotives on shed in the middle of the day, as Ahrons once wrote of the Midland Great Western, '*forty* engines out of a total stock of 139 on Broadstone shed!' At one time the Belfast–Holywood shuttle service was worked by steam railmotors, providing a regular interval service of about 25 minutes throughout the day.

For the main line service to Downpatrick and Newcastle the BNCR followed the lead of its neighbour across the lough and obtained its locomotives from Beyer Peacock & Co. The passenger locomotives were of the 2-4-0 type, two-cylinder compounds, identical save for a few unimportant details to the 'light compound' 2-4-0s of the Belfast & Northern Counties, and can thus be credited to Bowman Malcolm. They carried the coat of arms of the company on the side panels of the cab and on the tender, but otherwise gave no indication of their ownership. They were very smartly turned out in dark green, while the driving wheel splashers were adorned with Beyer Peacock's elaborate brass maker's plate. The three locomotives of this class worked on the Belfast–Newcastle trains, which took about $1\frac{1}{2}$ hours for the 38-mile journey when most of the intermediate stops were called. They survived the first world war, but not for long. The last of them was scrapped in 1922. Unlike the Belfast & Northern Counties, the 'County Down' did not name any of its locomotives.

Another considerably less elegant class that also just survived the war was one of four 4-4-2 tank engines of most ungainly appearance. In the 1890s the need was apparently felt for a powerful engine for the Bangor line and it seems that the design was left to Beyer Peacock. They were built as Worsdell von Borries compounds with the 2-4-2 wheel arrangement, with a very long rigid wheelbase – 8ft 5in plus 8ft 9in plus 7ft 3in. The coupled wheels were only 5ft 1in diameter, but the carrying wheels were as large as 4ft 0in. The positioning of the dome on the rearmost ring of a three-ring boiler barrel did not improve the appearance. Like the BNCR compounds they had Walschaerts valve gear for cylinders of the same size as Bowman Malcolm's 'heavy compounds' on the BNCR. They were soon in trouble from their long rigid wheelbase, and after about two years work they were fitted with a leading bogie having outside frames. Between 1903 and 1905 they were converted into simple engines.

For the lighter branch line services a smart little 2-4-2 type of quite conventional design, of tank engine was introduced in 1896, very similar in appearance to F. W. Webb's 2-4-2 tanks on the LNWR. They had 16in by 24in cylinders, and 5ft 6in coupled wheels, and appear to have been excellent locomotives for their size. They had an unexpectedly long life. In 1904 the BCDR joined in the fashion then prevailing on many British railways in purchasing or building for themselves steam railmotors for dealing economically with branch line and short commuter runs at off-peak periods. The BNCR had in mind particularly the Bangor line, where there was a day-long traffic between Belfast and Holywood, only four miles, while business was not so heavy to and from the outer stations except at commuter times. Three railmotors were purchased from Kitson & Co, of the type most generally favoured, namely a locomotive of the 0-4-0 type attached at one end of a saloon car, forming one of the bogies. Like all such units they had the disadvantage that when the locomotive was withdrawn for repairs the car itself was unusable. The railmotors were withdrawn in 1918, and the small 0-4-0 locomotives scrapped, whereupon the 2-4-2 tank engines were equipped for push-and-pull auto-train working and took over the Belfast–Holywood service.

For the main line an important change in motive power policy came in 1901. In England, on the London Tilbury & Southend Railway, it had been shown how successfully a short-distance main line could be operated almost entirely by tank engines. The locomotive superintendent, R. G. Miller adopted the 4-4-2 type, but in a very different form to the ill-starred compounds, that had begun life as 2-4-2s. The new locomotives of 1901 were as simple, straightforward and handsomely styled as the earlier ones were not, though they retained one feature in having the dome on the rearmost of a 3-ring boiler barrel. There were eventually 12 of this class, varying in successive batches as to boiler details, but all having the same basic dimensions: cylinders 17in by 24in, coupled wheels 5ft 6in and boiler pressure of 160lb/sq in. They were all built by Beyer Peacock & Co, but the size of the side tanks precluded the use of that firm's famous builder's plate, traditionally over the leading coupled wheel splasher.

Their running numbers were scattered as far as possible, one could imagine, over the full range of 30 locomotives. The first three, delivered in 1901 were, in order of building Nos 30, 3 and 15; then two more came in 1904, Nos 11 and 12. These five had round-topped fireboxes, but the next batch (Nos 1, 17 and 20) delivered in 1909 had Belpaire fireboxes and pressure increased to 175lb/sq in. They proved excellent for the curves and gradients of the line to Newcastle. At one time there were trains running non-stop over the 38 miles from Belfast to Newcastle in 50 minutes, and these tank engines coped with this assignment admirably. The loads were not very heavy, consisting of six-wheeled stock. When the time came for another four of these locomotives to be purchased in 1921 there was a slight re-arrangement of the tubes reducing the total heating surface to 1069.7sq ft from the original 1130sq ft, and the boiler pressure was reduced again to 160lb/sq in. As with all locomotives on the BCDR, they were non-superheated. The numbers of the 1921 batch of 4-4-2 tanks were equally scattered, namely 13, 18, 19 and 21.

Before their introduction there had been a change in locomotive superintendents in 1919. In that year R. G. Miller, who had held the job since 1880, retired and was succeeded by J. L. Crosthwait who had been district locomotive superintendent at Waterford, on the GSWR. He was a brother of H. W. Crosthwait who had been locomotive running superintendent at Inchicore headquarters in Watson's time. It had evidently been found that the original 4-4-2 tanks with 160lb/sq in pressure could do all that was necessary on the Newcastle trains, and the boiler pressure was reduced in order to economise in boiler maintenance costs. Crosthwait signalised his arrival on the BCDR by the introduction of the very handsome 4-6-4 tank engines, which came from Beyer Peacock & Co in 1920. A more powerful locomotive was needed for the smartly-timed residential trains on the Bangor line, and a writer in *The Railway Magazine* stated that the new ones were not only built but designed by Beyer Peacock, no mention whatever being made of Crosthwait. When related to locomotives the word 'design' can have a somewhat ambiguous meaning, according to whether one is referring to the individual who lays down the specification, and is responsible to the railway management for the production and working of the locomotives, or to the many draughtsmen making the drawings from which they are built. In the case of an entirely new design like the BCDR 4-6-4s I can well imagine that a large number of new drawings were needed, far beyond the capacity of the Belfast drawing office to produce, but one cannot claim that the design of the engine was due to Beyer Peacock, any more than could attribute the 'Royal Scots' of the LMS to the North British Locomotive Company.

Crosthwait's 4-6-4 tanks had 19in by 26in outside cylinders with Walschaerts valve gear, and 5ft 6in coupled wheels. Although the 4-4-2 tanks that preceeded them all had Stephenson's link motion, the Walschaerts gear was not new on the 'County Down' because the compound engines, like their counterparts on the Belfast & Northern Counties also had it. The new 4-6-4 tank engines were very handsome. They had a total heating surface of 1621.7sq ft, a grate area of 24.7 sq ft, and carried a boiler pressure of 170lb/sq in. Although the adhesion weight was no more than 45.5 tons their all-up weight, concentrated in a relatively short wheelbase, precluded their use from other than the Bangor line, but there the ample tractive effort was well employed in working the heavy residential trains.

Like all other BCDR locomotives, they were not superheated.

Although the Bangor line is no more than 12¼ miles long and never far from the shores of Belfast Lough, it includes some steep gradients, up to 1 in 73, and much curvature that precludes any fast running. I never travelled on the line, but in the later 1930s when I was frequently in Northern Ireland I used to go over to Queens Quay station to watch the trains coming and going. The homeward rush in the evenings began with the 5.15pm, first stop St Helens Bay, nine miles in 17 minutes, and reaching Bangor 10 minutes later. The 5.25pm all stations to Craigavad followed, completing the 6½ miles in 17 minutes with four intermediate stops; then followed the 5.45pm, 5.50pm, and 6.10pm and 6.20pm semi-fasts, of which the 6.10pm was non-stop to Bangor in 20 minutes. At the same time, leaving Queens Quay there was the 5.40pm to Newcastle, 5.48pm to Donaghadee, and the 6.14pm to Downpatrick, not to mention push-and-pull 'motors' to Holywood at 4.55pm and 6.00pm. The 5.40pm to Newcastle made its first stop at Crossgar, 21¼ miles out, in 30 minutes, reaching Newcastle at 6.40pm. The fastest trains on that line were the Afternoon Excursion Expresses on certain days of the week during the summer season. They left Queens Quay at 2.30pm and ran non-stop to Newcastle in an hour, and returned at 8.45pm; they were very popular, and frequently loaded up to 15 six-wheeled coaches, for the return fare was one shilling and sixpence (7½p).

On these trains the two large 0-6-0 goods tender locomotives were used. These were No 10 (1914) and No 4 (1921); they differed slightly as to boiler dimensions but had 18in by 26in cylinders and 5ft 0in wheels. The earlier one had 1438sq ft of heating surface, and carried a pressure of 170lb/sq in, while the second had 1367sq ft and the reduced pressure of 160lb/sq in that Mr Crosthwait favoured. The weight of the locomotives was 44 tons, and the tender with 2500 gallons of water and four tons of coal, 28¾ tons. Alike in outward appearance they were fine massive-looking machines, and had a reasonable turn of speed in addition to an ability to climb the severe gradients of the Newcastle line, with the heavy excursion trains. The two remaining 0-6-0s, Nos 14 and 26, were similar in general appearance to the two large ones, but had smaller boilers. No 14, dating from 1904, is interesting as being the first on the line to have a Belpaire firebox. No 26, dating from 1892, was rebuilt to conform in 1921. They had 17in by 24in cylinders, and the usual 160lb/sq in pressure. As in the later pair, the coupled wheels were 5ft 0in.

The last replacements in the capital list of steam locomotives to maintain the stock at 30 took place in 1924–5. In the former year the 0-4-2 tank No 16 was scrapped, and shortly after there went No 8, one of the 2-4-2 tanks. These two were replaced by a larger version of the popular 4-4-2 tank, carrying the same numbers as those scrapped. They had 5ft 6in coupled wheels, 18in by 26in cylinders, and a large boiler with heating surface of 1375sq ft with grate area of 20sq ft. They had a larger tank capacity than the earlier 4-4-2 tanks, 2000 gallons as against 1600, and carrying four tons of coal instead of three. With a boiler pressure of 170lb/sq in, they were considerably more powerful, but owing to their weight they were limited to the Bangor line. The leading dimensions of the three principal classes of passenger tank engine in the period under review may be compared thus:

BCDR PASSENGER TANK LOCOMOTIVES

Type	4-4-2	4-4-2	4-6-4
Year introduced	1901	1924	1920
Cylinders: dia in	17	18	19
stroke in	24	26	26
Coupled wheel dia ft in	5 6	5 6	5 6
Heating surface sq ft	1069.7	1375	1621.7
Grate area, sq ft	18	20	24.7
Pressure, lb/sq in	160	170	170
Total weight, tons	56.65	66	81.6
Tractive effort, lb at 85% boiler pressure	14,220	18,370	20,450

The locomotive stock of the BCDR after the addition of the two large 4-4-2 tanks can be listed as follows:

No	Type	Description	Year built or rebuilt
1	4-4-2T	17-inch	1909
2	0-4-2T	Shunting	1902
3	4-4-2T	17-inch	1901

No	Type	Description	Year built or rebuilt
4	0–6–0	18-inch	1914
5	2–4–2T	Push-pull trains	1896
6	2–4–0	Non-compound	1894
7	2–4–2T	Push-pull trains	1896
8	4–4–2T	18-inch	1924
9	0–4–2T	Shunting	1900
10	0–6–0	18-inch	1921
11	4–4–2T	17-inch	1904
12	4–4–2T	17-inch	1904
13	4–4–2T	17-inch	1921
14	0–6–0	18-inch	1904
15	4–4–2T	17-inch	1901
16	4–4–2T	18-inch	1924
17	4–4–2T	17-inch	1909
18	4–4–2T	17-inch	1921
19	4–4–2T	17-inch	1921
20	4–4–2T	17-inch	1909
21	4–4–2T	17-inch	1921
22	4–6–4T	19-inch	1920
23	4–6–4T	19-inch	1920
24	4–6–4T	19-inch	1920
25	4–6–4T	19-inch	1920
26	0–6–0	17-inch	1892
27	2–4–2T	Push-pull trains	1897
28	2–4–2T	Push-pull trains	1897
29	0–6–4T	Shunting	1923
30	4–4–2T	17-inch	1901

CHAPTER 8

Northern Counties Committee:
Compounds to Superheater 4-4-0s

At the time of Bowman Malcolm's retirement in September 1922 the passenger locomotive stock of the NCC consisted of three early 2-4-0 simples, four superheater 4-4-0 simples, and 27 compounds of the 2-cylinder Worsdell-von-Borries type, as follows:

Class	Type	Cylinders			Coupled	Boiler	Number
		HP dia in	LP dia in	stroke in	wheel dia ft in	pressure lb/sq in	built
A	4-4-0	18	26	24	6 0	175	13
B	4-4-0	16	23¼	24	6 0	160	5
C	2-4-0	16	23¼	24	6 0	160	7
D	4-4-0	18	26	24	7 0	170	2

Actually the class letters did not correspond with the order of production, for the dates of the first built of each class were A 1901, B 1897, C 1890, and D 1895. The last-mentioned were originally built as 2-4-0s, but were converted to 4-4-0s in 1897. In addition to Malcolm's own locomotives there were in 1922 four old 2-4-0 simples of Sharp Stewart build dating from 1856, but which had been much rebuilt subsequently. In their final state they had 15in by 22in cylinders and coupled wheels of 5ft 7½in. The stud was completed by nine Beyer Peacock 2-4-0s dating from 1872, with outside frames, and smokebox wings — sturdy, handsome locomotives, with 16in by 22in cylinders. All nine were still in service in 1922, though the last had been scrapped before my own first visit to the NCC in 1935.

All 27 two-cylinder compound passenger locomotives included in the foregoing table had inside Walschaerts valve gear, and on Malcolm's first two superheated simple 4-4-0s built in 1914 the same gear was used. These fine locomotives, the first entirely new type to be introduced since the Midland take-over, were considered to have evidence of Derby influences, but really if one excepts the purely superficial feature of the shape of the running plate over the coupled wheel centres there was nothing at all, particularly in Bowman Malcolm's continued use of the Walschaerts valve gear. They had the characteristic long wheelbase bogie of the previous 'heavy compound' 4-4-0s, and outside frames on the tenders. There was a beautiful example of an F. Moore coloured plate of one of them in *The Railway Magazine* of June 1917. Two more were added to stock in 1922 just before Malcolm retired. They were followed by three 0-6-0 goods locomotives, which had the same boiler, cylinders and motion (Walschaerts gear) and coupled wheels 5ft 2½in. They were put into traffic in 1923. Malcolm's earlier 0-6-0s had been two-cylinder compounds.

In 1924 the Midlandisation of the locomotive stock began to be more pronounced, but it was by no means absolute. In that year a new batch of superheater 4-4-0s was authorised; while so far as wheelbase and machinery were concerned they were the same as the preceeding locomotives of Malcolm's design they had the Midland standard boiler as fitted to the superheated rebuilt Class 2P 4-4-0s. Comparative dimensions of the two varieties were:

NCC SUPERHEATER 4–4–0s

Date introduced	1914	1924
Class	U	U2
Cylinders, in	19×24	19×24
Coupled wheels, ft in	6 0	6 0
Boiler pressure, lb/sq in	170	170
Heating surface, sq in:		
Tubes	876	1045
Firebox	110.5	123
Superheater	275	253
Total	1261.5	1421
Grate area, sq ft	18	21.8
Locomotive weight, tons	47.6	50.45
Locomotive and tender, tons	76.85	83.3

A total of 10 of the new 4-4-0s were authorised. Three, Nos 79, 80 and 81 were built in Belfast, the remainder by the North British Locomotive Company. The tender, in which the traditional outside frames were at last abandoned, had a very Midland look, though it was much smaller than those being currently fitted to the smaller locomotives on the parent system. Carrying six tons of coal and only 2500 gallons of water its all-up weight was no more than $32\frac{3}{4}$ tons, as compared to the $41\frac{1}{4}$ tons of those fitted to the LMS Class 2P 4-4-0s. The cab, dome cover, and chimney were pure Midland, while an additional Derby feature was the Fowler & Anderson by-pass valve on the cylinders. This fitting was subsequently removed.

The process of modernising the passenger locomotive stock had begun even before Malcolm retired. The five 'light compound' 4-4-0s of the B Class, numbered 24, 59, 60, 61 and 62, had for some time been employed on the Belfast–Larne line. They were elegant little things, characterised externally by the relatively short coupled wheelbase of only 7ft 0in and the striding effect of the long wheelbase of the bogie, 6ft 6in. But with small cylinders and a boiler pressure of no more than 160lb/sq in the nominal tractive effort was only 11,560lb at 85 percent boiler pressure. In 1921 Malcolm rebuilt Nos 60 and 61 with larger boilers, increasing the heating surface from 793.12sq ft to 936.27sq ft and increasing the pressure to 170lb/sq in, which put the tractive effort up to 12,282lb. This rebuilding was very successful, and the two locomotives worked relatively heavy trains between Belfast and Larne with good economy. It is sometimes the case when locomotives are rebuilt with larger boilers that the thermal efficiency of their working suffers, but this was certainly not the case with Nos 60 and 61. They remained compounds, and not superheated.

With loads continuing to increase, Mr Wallace and his locomotive assistant H. P. Stewart decided to try a more substantial rebuild of two more of this class, Nos 59 and 62. The frames were good, and the motion was in good condition, so they were rebuilt as two-cylinder simples. Sound though the frames were, it was not considered they would be strong enough to support a tractive effort of 17,860lb which would have resulted from use of 19in by 24in cylinders as on Malcolm's superheater 4-4-0s of Class U and on the new 4-4-0s of Class U2 then under construction both in Belfast and Glasgow. So a compromise was made, using the Midland Class 2 boiler superheated, but with 18in by 24in cylinders. The resulting tractive effort was

16,065lb. Even so, this was a boost of nearly 40 percent above the original 11,560lb on the Class B light compounds, and the frames stood up to it admirably. The water capacity of the original tender was increased by raising the sides, and with 2500 gallons, instead of 2090 gallons, and six tons of coal, no difficulty was experienced in working the non-stop Portrush expresses. At that time the Greenisland direct line giving a through run from Belfast towards Portrush and Londonderry had not been built, and the actual non-stop run was one of 61 miles, from the point of direction-reversal at Greenisland itself. These locomotives were classed as U1, and despite their strong 'Midland' look could be readily distinguished from U2 by the retention of the original frames and running plates, and by their outside framed tenders. They retained also evidence of their Beyer Peacock ancestry in the traditional brass beading over the driving wheel splashers.

Before renewal of the remaining stud of compound passenger locomotives began in 1926 there was one isolated locomotive that must be mentioned. This was the last of the five original light compound 4-4-0s, No 24. When Malcolm reboilered Nos 60 and 61, while retaining compound working, a third boiler was built, and this was eventually used in a kind of 'half-way-house' rebuild of No 24, which was converted from compound to simple, with 18in by 24in cylinders, and had the non-superheated spare boiler fitted. This locomotive was used on short-distance and secondary duties. Conversions from compound began in earnest in 1926 when two further light compounds, this time of the 2-4-0 type, were rebuilt to correspond with the rebuilt 4-4-0s Nos 59 and 62. This involved considerably more work, as the frames had to be lengthened at the front end, and bogies provided. One of the two converted was No 33 Galgorm Castle, which at first retained its name carried on the Beyer Peacock splasher after rebuilding. When the systematic naming scheme for the entire passenger locomotive stud began in 1931 the name was transferred to one of the surviving 2-4-0 compounds.

The LMS had a smaller standard superheated boiler known as the G6s, which was later used on the Fowler 2-6-2 tank engines, and in continuing the rebuilding of the compounds this boiler was used for most of the remainder. Although the ultimate result was the same as far as tractive power was concerned, the rebuilt locomotives were segregated into distinct classes according to whether they had originally been 'light' or 'heavy' compounds. They were subsequently known as classes B3 and A1 respectively. The boilers on both had a total heating surface, including superheater, of 1038sq ft while the grate area was $17\frac{3}{4}$sq ft. The cylinders were 18in by 24in as on Class U1. It was a curious system of classification. At first thought it might have seemed a way of distinguishing between locomotives having the same outward appearance, but having different frame structures arising from the original light and heavy compounds. Both A1 and B3 classes had the same loading limits, and the obscurity was made even more inexplicable in that locomotives of *both* classes had boilers working at 200lb/sq in instead of 170lb/sq in. The nominal tractive effort of the A1 and B3 locomotives with 200lb/sq in pressure actually became greater than that of the new ones with 19in cylinders.

When the Greenisland loop line was opened, and in its 1 in $76\frac{1}{2}$ provided the most severe ascent on the main lines of the Committee, the 4-4-0s were grouped into two categories of loading and they seemed to have been based on boiler heating surface and grate area, rather than tractive efforts.

4–4–0 LOCOMOTIVE LOADINGS

Class	Description	Boiler pressure, lb/sq in	Nominal tractive effort, lb	Load, tons
A1	Rebuilt from heavy compound	170	16,065	235
A1	Rebuilt from heavy compound	200	18,900	235
B3	Rebuilt from light compound	170	16,065	235
B3	Rebuilt from light compound	200	18,900	235
U	Superheated locomotives of 1914 design	170	17,860	235
U1	Rebuilt from light compound LMS Class 2 boiler	170	16,065	255
U2	New locomotives of 1924	170	17,860	255

As the rebuilding moved towards completion, in the wave of tremendous enterprise and publicity generated under the management of Major M. S. Speir in the 1930s, the four classes of 4-4-0s were given names: A1 became the Mountains, B3 the Counties, U1 the Glens, and U2 the Castles. The U Class of 1914

Plate 11(a) Ex-Dublin & South Eastern 2—4—2 tank No 439 (formerly No 40, built at Grand Canal Street in 1902); scrapped 1952. (*L&GRP*)

(b) Ex-Dublin & South Eastern 4—4—2 tank No 455 (formerly No 20 *King George*, built at Grand Canal Street in 1911); scrapped 1959. (*L&GRP*)

Plate 12(a) Ex-Dublin & South Eastern 2–6–0 express goods locomotive No 461 (formerly No 15, built by Beyer Peacock & Co in 1922). This was withdrawn from service in 1965, and is now preserved.

(b) J. R. Bazin's prototype 2–6–2 tank No 850, built at Inchicore in 1928. The design was never multiplied. It was withdrawn in 1955. (*H. C. Casserley*)

was excluded, because the locomotives were in process of being converted to Castles. The two 7ft 0in compounds built in 1895 are not included in the above classification. No 50 *Jubilee* had been rebuilt in 1926 as a two-cylinder simple, with a boiler of the same dimensions as the U Class and 19in by 24in cylinders. Because of its 7ft 0in coupled wheels its tractive effort was only 15,300lb and it was rated with the 235-ton group. On the only times that I saw it, the locomotive was acting as yard pilot at Belfast running shed. Its one-time sister, No 55 *Parkmount*, remained a compound to the very end. In 1939 No 50 was still working on the Limavady branch. In their very original state as 2-4-0s they bore an almost uncanny likeness to the Webb Precedent class 2-4-0s on the LNWR except of course for their outside-framed tenders.

As rebuilt, named, and in many cases re-numbered, the compounds were as follows:

New No	Name	Original No	Original type	Class
GLEN SERIES: NEW CLASS U1				
1	*Glenshesk*	59	4-4-0	B
2	*Glendun*	62	4-4-0	B
3	*Glenaan*	33	2-4-0	C
4	*Glenariff*	52	2-4-0	C
COUNTY SERIES: NEW CLASS B3				
21	*County Down*	51	2-4-0	C
24	*County Londonderry*	24	4-4-0	B
28	*County Tyrone*	58	2-4-0	C
60	*County Donegal*	60	4-4-0	B
61	*County Antrim*	61	4-4-0	B
MOUNTAIN SERIES: NEW CLASS A1				
33	*Binevenagh*	3	4-4-0	A
34	*Knocklayd*	34	4-4-0	A
58	—	17	4-4-0	A
62	*Slemish*	4	4-4-0	A
64	*Trostan*	64	4-4-0	A
65	*Knockagh*	65	4-4-0	A
66	*Ben Madigan*	66	4-4-0	A
68	*Slieve Gallion*	68	4-4-0	A
69	*Slieve Bane*	9	4-4-0	A

New No	Name	Original No	Original type	Class
ASSIMILATED TO CASTLE CLASS: U2				
84	*Lisanoure Castle*	20	4-4-0	A
85	—	67	4-4-0	A
86	—	5	4-4-0	A
87	*Queen Alexandra*	63	4-4-0	A
70	—	70	4-4-0	U*
71	*Glenarm Castle*	71	4-4-0	U*

*Not compounds originally

The ten locomotives of Class U2 built new in 1924 were named as follows:

74	*Dunluce Castle*	79	*Kenbaan Castle*
75	*Antrim Castle*	80	*Dunseverick Castle*
76	*Olderfleet Castle*	81	*Carrickfergus Castle*
77	(no name)	82	*Dunananie Castle*
78	*Chichester Castle*	83	*Carra Castle*

The last of the Class A heavy compounds, No 63 *Queen Alexandra*, was not rebuilt until 1936. Before that it had been stationed at Cookstown, and at that time the small shed there was unusual in housing none but two-cylinder compounds. The other two were Class C 2-4-0 light compounds. There was certainly some NCC history, or perhaps more correctly BNCR history, in the trio of locomotives at Cookstown in the 1930s, though only the 4-4-0 No 63 was in its original condition. The 2-4-0s, then numbered 51 and 57, had both been rebuilt with larger boilers, though remaining as compounds. No 51 was the pioneer of the entire compound fleet on the BNCR as it was originally No 21; its companion at Cookstown carried the name borne by the second 2-4-0 compound, *Galgorm Castle*. The latter, No 33, was rebuilt as a class U1. At first it carried its old name, but when the U1s were given the class name of Glens, No 33, which had been renumbered 3 was renamed *Glenaan*, and the name *Galgorm Castle* was transferred to No 57, another of the original 2-4-0 light compounds. In 1935 it was regularly working the 12.40pm through train from Cookstown to Belfast, returning with the 4.20pm, and on the latter duty I had the pleasure of riding on the footplate.

On that occasion I did not go into Cookstown, but at the junction of Magherafelt transferred to the other compound, No 51, to ride up the Derry Central line to Coleraine before returning passenger; it was not until a snowy day in December 1935 that I made my way to Cookstown itself. Then, on coming to Magherafelt I found that for the last part of the journey our locomotive was to be the last remaining Class A heavy compound *Queen Alexandra*. I was no less interested to see that it still carried the old 'invisible green' livery, at a time when almost every other NCC locomotive was resplendent and beautifully turned-out in Midland red. On arrival at Cookstown I photographed it in the snow, nicely posed on the turntable, but in the weak winter light the result was a bit gloomy. The picture does show that in spite of the age of the paintwork the locomotive was nicely polished, and the lining-out was clear. It could not have been six months later that I went to Belfast and saw it again, a glittering apparition in Midland red, newly out of the works, transformed into a U2 and numbered 87, but still named *Queen Alexandra*.

The three remaining 2-4-0 compounds were fascinating little things: No 56, with the original small boiler, was often bustling around Belfast yard, while Nos 51 and 57 had their regular turns from Cookstown. I shall never forget my footplate rides on these locomotives. It was like stepping on to one of the exhibits in York Railway Museum, except that there was a businesslike efficiency about their working that had nothing of the museum piece about them. I had never before, or since, ridden on anything as small as a 2-4-0. These locomotives unlike those of the Midland, started up full compound, except for the first stroke of the pistons during which live steam was admitted to the low-pressure cylinder. The moment the high-pressure cylinder exhausted, the changeover to compound working was automatic. This made them extremely simple to drive. Although they had a two-port regulator, the first port was used only for light steaming, as in the case of contemporary modern locomotives that were similarly equipped. They had lever reversing gear, and positioning of the lever adjusted the valve travel and associated cut-offs simultaneously in both high- and low-pressure cylinders. While the principles underlying such adjustments were simple enough the physical work could be strenuous. A regulator under steam took some

111

LMS (NCC): 4.20pm BELFAST–ANTRIM
Load: 3 coaches, 83 tons tare, 85 tons full
Locomotive: 2-cylinder compound No 57 *Galgorm Castle*

Miles	Locations	Schedule min	Actual min sec	Speeds mph	Regulator opening	Reverse lever	Cut-off% HP	LP
0.0	BELFAST (YORK ROAD)	0	0 00	—		Full	79	82
3.3	Whitehouse		5 25	49	$\frac{7}{8}$	3 back*	62	67
4.6	*Bleach Green Jcn*	7	7 10	44½	$\frac{7}{8}$	2 back	68½	73
7.0	Mossley		11 17	32	$\frac{7}{8}$	2 back	68½	73
8.2	BALLYCLARE JCN	14	13 30	39½	$\frac{7}{8}$	3 back	62	67
—			p.w.s.	15				
9.2	*Kingsbog Jcn*		14 50	—				
10.9	Doagh		17 13	57	$\frac{3}{4}$	3 back	62	67
13.9	Templepatrick		20 17	65	1st Valve	4 back	48	54
15.9	Dunadry	23½	22 48		1st Valve	4 back	48	54
0.0			0 00	—				
1.4	Muckamore		2 41	52½	Full	Full	79	82
3.4	ANTRIM	6	5 17	—	Full	then 4 back	48	54

*reverse moved to three notches back from full gear about ½-mile from start to Belfast.

shifting, and a notched lever reversing gear was worse. On *Galgorm Castle*, working the 4.20pm out of Belfast, both controls were being altered every few minutes, and the locomotive had been fitted with a steel plate on the front of the reversing rack, so that by putting one foot against it the driver could get more purchase on the lever.

Although the load of the 4.20pm train was one of no more than three bogie coaches, 85 tons all told, it was about the same as that of the English Mail on the GS&WR at the time the Aspinall 60 Class of 4-4-0s were in their prime between Dublin and Cork. Moreover, on the first stage out of Belfast the train had to run up to the standard of the 80-minute Portrush expresses. Indeed, from each of the starts, and we called at all stations after Antrim, I was treated to the rare spectacle of a locomotive being driven absolutely all out – full regulator and full forward gear. As we worked into speed the two exhausts per revolution from the low-pressure cylinder became tremendous. The accompanying log of the run as far as Antrim is so far as I know the only detailed record of the working of these compounds, which held the fort for so long on the NCC. By way of explanation the line is level as far as Whitehouse, and at this point we had attained a speed of 49mph. The ascent to Ballyclare Junction begins with $1\frac{1}{4}$ miles at 1 in 102, and then it is 1 in $76\frac{1}{2}$ for three miles, followed by $\frac{1}{2}$-mile at 1 in 89 almost to the junction.

The timing of 14 minutes for this initial 8.2 miles certainly leaves nothing to spare, and with the Portrush expresses time was frequently dropped, to be regained later in the journey. But the little 2-4-0 did not fall below 32mph on the 1 in $76\frac{1}{2}$ gradient, and observing the severe temporary speed restriction at the actual summit the locomotive was taken fast down to the first stop at Dunadry. Riding on a 2-4-0 at a speed of 60mph can be a rather tempestuous experience. Those who have ridden on the LNWR Precedents and the famous Gladstone 0-4-2s of the Brighton have described the action set up when crossing points at speed as galloping. *Galgorm Castle* did not do this; it kept up a peculiar bouncing action, and at the slightest curve added a hearty sideways roll! At 65mph this was quite an experience. There was some very smart running on the branch, as shown in the following summary times:

Section	Distance miles	Time min sec	Maximum speed, mph
Cookstown Jcn-Randalstown	2	4 17	48
Randalstown-Staffordstown	5½	8 22	57½
Staffordstown-Toome	3¾	5 43	58½
Toome-Castledawson	4¼	6 35	—
Castledawson-Magherafelt	2¼	4 41	—

On a summer evening of almost cloudless sunshine it was a delightful run, so near to the northern shores of Lough Neagh. The continuation northwards to Coleraine up the Derry Central line on No 51 was equally enjoyable, though with only two coaches and a less exacting schedule the work required from locomotive and crew was not so demanding.

Before finishing with the compounds, I must mention the two 0-6-0s built by Bowman Malcolm in 1892. Freight traffic on the NCC and on the BNCR before was never very heavy, and it seemed to be a regular thing to have locomotives that could deal equally with passenger and goods. The two 0-6-0s anticipated, by nine years, the cylinder dimensions used on the heavy compound 4-4-0s, being 18in and 26in diameter, both with a stroke of 24in, with Walschaerts valve gear. In the mid-1930s, the second of these locomotives, No 54, was still in service as a compound. Bowman Malcolm also built three superheated 0-6-0s, Nos 13, 14, and 15, with 5ft 2½in wheels, and boiler, cylinders and motion the same as his U Class 4-4-0s. They were actually completed in February 1923, after he had retired. Though primarily intended for goods working they proved to have an excellent turn of speed, and they were used on intermediate passenger duties – in fact it was the only work on which I ever saw them engaged, on stopping trains on the Belfast–Larne route.

CHAPTER 9

Narrow Gauge
in the North-West and North

It would be difficult to imagine three railways so alike in the fascination of their locomotives and rolling stock, and so unalike in their financial circumstances and management status as the County Donegal, the Lough Swilly and the group of narrow gauge lines beneath the umbrella of the NCC. North-west Donegal must be one of the most thinly-populated regions in the whole of the British Isles. On the half-inch ordnance survey map covering most of the territory once served by the lines of the County Donegal Joint Committee Railway there are less than a dozen townships printed in bold type, and only one of these, Donegal itself, has a population of much over 1000. Even assuming that the object was to open-up the country it would not have seemed a very profitable place to do it, and had it not been for the rivalry between two major railways the 'County Donegal' might have languished into near-liquidation, as so many of the other Irish narrow gauge railways were fated to do.

By the turn of the century, with narrow gauge lines extending westwards from Stranorlar to Donegal and Killybegs, and a subsidiary line making a lonely, and rather hopeless way through desolate country to Glenties, such traffic as there was flowed towards Londonderry. Originally it was transhipped from narrow gauge to the broad gauge trains of the Great Northern at Strabane. The management of the Donegal Railway felt that this was not exactly an economic move for a journey of less than 15 miles, and in 1896 obtained Parliamentary section to build a narrow gauge line of its own on the opposite bank of the Foyle river to the line of the Great Northern, and so bring the produce direct into Londonderry, whence it went to England by sea. This was the situation that existed from August 1900, when the narrow gauge line from Strabane to Londonderry was opened. In 1903 the Midland Railway of England took over the Belfast & Northern Counties Railway, and in the expansionist spirit of the age made the first moves towards securing control of the Donegal Railway, which by that time was engaged in building a branch line of $15\frac{1}{4}$ miles from Donegal to Ballyshannon, a remote but charming watering place on the Atlantic coast.

The Great Northern, which was still smarting over the loss of the Donegal Railway traffic by the construction of the independent line between Strabane and Londonderry, had no desire to see the Midland Railway extending its tentacles into Donegal, especially as there would soon be a competitive point at Ballyshannon, through which the Bundoran line of the Great Northern passed on its way from the junction point with the Dundalk–Londonderry line. Negotiations resulted in the Donegal Railway passing into the joint ownership of the Midland and the GNR(I), by an Act of Amalgamation passed in May 1906. The controlling body became the County Donegal Railways Joint Committee, consisting of three representatives from each company. Because of the special position of the line between Strabane and Londonderry, parallel to a wholly-owned Great Northern broad gauge line, the narrow gauge line was handed over to the Midland Railway, to be worked by locomotives and stock of the Joint Committee. Backed henceforth by one of the most prosperous of the Irish railways, and by the vast capital and resources of the Midland, the County Donegal became the most fortunate of all the Irish narrow gauge lines.

It certainly needed all the luck that came its way. Just imagine the physical and geographical situation, apart from any problems of economics: from its nodal station and headquarters at Stranorlar, a 'main line' extending for 37 tortuous and steeply-graded miles through a remote and desolate country where the largest centres of population were Donegal itself and the terminus at Killybegs, with populations of 1270 and 570 respectively, and a branch line of $24\frac{1}{2}$ miles to reach that centre of teeming population, Glenties, with 360 inhabitants! Then from Donegal there was the Ballyshannon branch. After the first world war and the partition of Ireland, the establishment of the international frontier midway between Strabane and Stranorlar, cut off the railway headquarters from its principal source of supply of materials via Londonderry, and Donegal had in future to rely on goods sent in bonded containers from Dublin, and travelling through Northern Ireland to be transferred to the narrow gauge at Strabane. But the 'County Donegal' owes an immense debt of gratitude to the members of the joint committee who chose Henry Forbes to be its traffic manager and secretary in 1910; not only was he a very able railwayman, but he had a temperament and personality that took the difficult and daunting conditions as a challenge. The idea of an Irish narrow gauge railway making a profit in the inter-war years may well sound unbelievable, but Forbes achieved this, admittedly by the extensive use of diesel railcars. As will be told later, however, steam was not neglected.

At the time of the 1906 amalgamation the Donegal Railway had 15 locomotives, all except the three earliest of which lasted into the 1930s. These latter were little 2-4-0 tank engines built by Sharp Stewart & Co in 1881, and two at any rate had been out of service since 1905. The remaining 12 were:

Class	Type	Builder	Date	Cylinders in	Coupled wheel dia ft in
2	4–6–0T	Neilson	1893	14×20	3 6
3	4–4–4T	Neilson Reid	1902	14×20	4 0
4	4–6–4T	Nasmyth Wilson	1904	15×21	3 9

It was reported that the Class 4 locomotives were not very good for steaming, and although capable of taking a relatively heavy load were apt to be unreliable at times. But in 1907, when more locomotives were required the Joint Committee again went to Nasmyth Wilson, but these were to be of the 2-6-4 wheel arrangement. This time the boiler was the same as that of the Neilson Reid 4-4-4s, which had proved very successful, while having a greater adhesion weight. All locomotives on the line were named, and the 20 on the books at the time of Forbes arrival were as follows, bearing in mind that Nos 1 and 2 were out of service:

1	*Alice*		6	*Inver*
2	*Blanche*		7	*Finn*
3	*Lydia*		8	*Foyle*
4	*Meenglas*		9	*Columbkille*
5	*Drumboe*		10	*Sir James*

11	Hercules	16	Donegal
12	Eske	17	Glenties
13	Owenea	18	Killybegs
14	Erne	19	Letterkenny
15	Mourne	20	Raphoe

I may add that *Hercules* had no relation to the tractive power of the locomotive. It was the Christian name of one of the directors of the Donegal Railway.

Nos 16 to 20 proved by far the best that the railway had yet possessed, with cylinders 14in by 21in, coupled wheels 4ft 0in, and carried a boiler pressure of 175lb/sq in. The tractive effort was 12,700lb. The only trouble, which affected all the County Donegal locomotives, was that the tank capacity of only 1000 gallons involved taking water at intermediate stations on the longer runs. When authorisation was given in 1912 for three additional locomotives a request was made for tanks of 2000-gallon capacity. The County Donegal was fortunate in having as its engineer and locomotive superintendent R. M. Livesay, a professional engineer of high status, who was at the same time an essentially practical man for the running of the exiguous train service, and an inventor of no mean reputation. Utilising the expert designing capacity of the builders, again Nasmyth Wilson & Co, he specified the addition of a superheater – for the first time ever on a British narrow gauge locomotive – and by the expected economy in water consumption the tanks were limited to a capacity of 1500 gallons, while giving the length of run requiring 2000 gallons on a comparable locomotive using saturated steam. In the equipment were included two specialities of Livesey's own: forced-feed lubrication for the axleboxes and bogie centres, and a variable blastpipe. Other fittings, unusual on a narrow gauge locomotive, were a speed indicator and recorder, (doubtless to ensure that speed restrictions were not exceeded), and a pyrometer for indicating the superheat temperature.

It is interesting to compare the dimensions of these very notable locomotives with those of the saturated 2-6-4 tanks that preceded them, in view of the latter subsequently being fitted with superheaters. The new locomotives of 1912 were unquestionably the most advanced design for the narrow gauge that had then been seen in the British Isles, and they very quickly proved that their qualification was not only on paper. They immediately showed themselves capable of greatly improved haulage capacity over the non-superheated version, taking loads of 200 tons up the long gradients of 1 in 50 at speeds sometimes exceeding 20mph, but what was more important from the operating point of view, on 30 percent less water. It should have

CDRJC: 2–6–4 TANK LOCOMOTIVES

Class	5	5A
Date	1907	1912
Cylinders: dia, in	14	$15\frac{1}{2}$
stroke, in	21	21
Coupled wheel dia, ft in	4 0	4 0
Heating surface, sq ft		
Tubes	637	540
Firebox	76	76
Superheater	—	160
Boiler pressure, lb/sq in	175	160*
Coal, tons	$2\frac{1}{2}$	$2\frac{1}{2}$
Water, gallons	1000	1500
Grate area, sq ft	11.5	11.5
Max axle load, tons	9.0	10.4
Total weight, tons	43.5	50.4
Tractive effort at 85% pressure, lb	12,700	14,300

*subsequently increased to 175 lb/sq in

		Post-1937		Original
Class	No	Name	No	Name
5A	1	*Alice*	21	*Ballyshannon*
5A	2	*Blanche*	2A	*Stranorlar*
5A	3	*Lydia*	3A	*Strabane*
5	4	*Meenglas*	16	*Donegal*
5	5	*Drumboe*	17	*Glenties*
5	6	*Columcille*	18	*Killybegs*
5	7	*Finn*	19	*Letterkenny*
5	8	*Foyle*	20	*Raphoe*
4	9	*Eske*	12	*Eske*
4	10	*Owenea*	13	*Owenea*
4	11	*Erne*	14	*Erne*
4	12	*Mourne*	15	*Mourne*

been mentioned also that these locomotives had piston instead of slide valves and of a diameter large in relation to the size of the cylinders. The three were named *Ballyshannon, Stranorlar,* and *Strabane,* and numbered 21, 2A and 3A respectively.

Until the formation of the Joint Committee the locomotives of the Donegal Railway had been green, but signifying the change in management the livery was changed to black lined-out in red, and with the side tanks and bunkers set off by a broad multi-coloured surround of red, yellow, and red. The crest of the Joint Committee was carried on the bunker panel. The *Locomotive Magazine* of July 1912 carried a very fine colour plate of *Ballyshannon,* reproduced from an oil painting by F. Moore.

With the decline of traffic after the first world war and the introduction of petrol and then diesel railcars, there was no need for so many steam locomotives. The last of the little 2-4-0 tanks was scrapped in 1926, and most of the Class 2 locomotives were withdrawn, if not actually scrapped at about the same time. With the disappearance of the original Nos 1, 2 and 3 the Class 5A superheated 2-6-4s were renumbered, and took the names of the old locomotives in 1928. The two 4-4-4 tanks were scrapped in 1933, and in 1937 the remaining stock of 12 was renumbered. All that remained had by then been superheated; the stud is summarised on page 119.

In the renaming it was evident that the object was to get rid of the names which were those of stations on the line, to avoid misunderstandings! While Forbes remained in charge as Manager at Stranorlar and gradually introduced diesel railcars to take over many of the passenger services, there was no attempt to denigrate the remaining steam locomotives; in fact steam traction, which was needed for the heavy mixed trains, was given a heartening boost in the late 1930s, when a change in the livery was made from black to a striking and spectacular pinkish-red, officially referred to as 'geranium'.

Forbes was still in office at the time of his sudden death, in 1943 after having been chief executive officer of the 'County Donegal' for 33 years. He took office at a critical time, but he loved and lived for the railway in all its aspects, steam and diesel alike, and he left it flourishing, showing a profit of 25 per cent of the total annual takings. There were certainly no finer narrow gauge steam locomotives than the three 5As, *Alice, Blanche* and

Lydia, which after their boiler pressure was increased to 175lb/sq in had a hefty tractive effort for 3ft 0in gauge locomotives of 15,650lb. To see one of these in its 'geranium' livery pounding up through Barnesmore Gap with a heavy mixed train was one of the railway sights of the British Isles.

I was no more than a schoolboy in his early teens when I became a regular subscriber to *The Railway Magazine* and one of the earliest issues that came my way, in February 1919 to be exact, had a lengthy article about a railway of which I had never previously heard, the Londonderry & Lough Swilly; it followed immediately after the frontispiece plate of an apparently very large and imposing 4-8-4 tank engine. The article itself did not attract me at the time. The only pictures apart from portraits were of singularly unattractive station buildings and goods sheds in Londonderry itself. I cannot remember ever reading the article or even referring back to it when more recent and attractively illustrated articles appeared in the same journal. It was not until I first went to Londonderry, crossed the Craigavon bridge and made my way along Strand Road to the station named Graving Dock that I turned up that old article again. I was puzzled, because although it was written in the first person there was no indication of the authorship. I did not recognise the style of any of the regular contributors to *The Railway Magazine*, but later guessed that it could well have been Joseph Tatlow, then a Director of the Midland Great Western Railway, whose autobiography was published by *The Railway Gazette* about the same time.

In April 1917 Tatlow had been asked by the Chairman of the Irish Board of Works to make an enquiry into the affairs of the Letterkenny & Burtonport Extension Railway, which was worked by the 'Lough Swilly'. During the war the lough itself, lengthy and well sheltered, was very active as a naval base; with Buncrana on one shore and Rathmullan opposite, as headquarters the whole area was teeming with service personnel, and the railway prospered. But it was far otherwise with the Burtonport extension, and of this Tatlow wrote:

Everything has for years past been allowed to run down; the direction and management have been characterised by extreme parsimony; and the disabled condition of the engines is undoubtedly due to lack of proper upkeep, which must have been going on for years. The state of the permanent way shows a want of proper maintenance; and the condition of the stations, buildings and of the carriages speaks of neglect.

It was not only the Burtonport extension that had fallen into a state of decrepitude and demoralisation. As that anonymous article in *The Railway Magazine* opened:

> Enough to say that time was when the railway appeared to exist as little more than a joke. Every wag with a good railway anecdote fired it off at the expense of the Lough Swilly. If you ever heard of the driver who stopped his train on a steep up gradient every morning to get his half-pint of milk from a wayside peasant's cottage, he was certain to be a Lough Swilly driver. And the doggy guard, accustomed to carrying along a famous fighting terrier or game cock and stop the train at any point where a challenger could be found was of course a Lough Swilly guard.

Reform on the Lough Swilly itself had begun in September 1916 with the appointment of Mr H. Hunt, from the Great Central as secretary and general manager, and he was made manager, under an Order of the Privy Council of the Letterkenny & Burtonport Extension Railway in July 1917. In two years from then, as Tatlow wrote in his autobiography:

> Trains are punctual now, engines do not break down, carriages are comfortable, goods traffic is well worked, and delays are exceptional. Much has been done, more would have been done but for difficulties due to the war, and a good deal still remains to be done.

No additions to the stock of steam locomotives had been made since 1912, and the situation in 1919 can be summarised as follows:

Locomotive numbers	Type	Date built	Builder	Cylinders dia×stroke, in	Coupled wheel dia ft in
1–4	4–6–0T	1902	Andrew Barclay	14×20	3 9
5–6*	4–6–2T	1899	Hudswell Clark	15×22	3 9
7–8	4–6–2T	1901	Hudswell Clark	15×22	3 9

*Renumbered 15 and 16 in 1913

Locomotive numbers	Type	Date built	Builder	Cylinders dia×stroke, in	Coupled wheel dia ft in
9–10	4–6–2T	1904	Kerr Stuart	14×20	3 6
11–12	4–8–0	1905	Hudswell Clark	15½×22	3 9
13–14	4–6–2T	1910	Hawthorn Leslie	14½×22	3 9
5–6	4–8–4T	1912	Hudswell Clark	16×20	3 9

There was also an old 0-6-0 tank built in 1885 by Black Hawthorn & Co, No 4 *Innishowen*, which was renumbered 17 in 1913, but it did little work after about 1925.

The 4-6-0 tank engines Nos 1 to 4 were lettered L&BER and were ordered by the Irish Board of Works in Dublin to specifications and tests laid down by their Engineer-in-Chief, T. M. Batchen. In fact although were so lettered they were used indiscriminately with other Lough Swilly stock. Apparently earmarked for the Letterkenny & Burtonport Extension, they would seem to have been anything but suitable for this line, 50 miles long through desolate country, if for no other reason than the limited water capacity of their side tanks, only 750 gallons. But at least one connoisseur of Irish locomotives considers they were the best the railway ever had. Whether this opinion was based on performance on the Burtonport extension, or elsewhere, I do not know. The 4-6-2 tanks were the most numerous, amounting to almost half the total locomotive stock of the line, in 1919. The three trains a day between Londonderry and Burtonport before the first world war took about 4½ hours for the journey of 74 miles with stops at all stations, but as the trains were mixed and involved the attaching and detaching of goods vehicles intermediately this time was often considerably exceeded.

The Burtonport line was no joke of a ride for locomotives or men. It was beyond Letterkenny that the really tough conditions began, with ruling gradients of 1 in 50 in the ensuing 20 miles westward to Creeslough, and then from Dunfanaghy Road the four-mile climb at an unbroken 1 in 50 to the summit 50¼ miles from Londonderry, 474ft above sea level. This was certainly no line for weak or ill-maintained locomotives, and one can well imagine that in the state of neglect that Tatlow refers to in his first report the situation could easily become quite chaotic. The highly-praised Andrew Barclay 4-6-0 tanks of 1902 had a nominal tractive effort of 12,000lb, but with their small tanks, and carrying no more than 1¼ tons of coal they must have had their limitations, and it was to work heavy mixed trains through over the 74 miles between Londonderry and Burtonport that the two 4-8-0 tender locomotives were obtained from Hudswell Clark & Co in 1905. These enabled a high tractive effort to be obtained with a very light axle-loading, and at the same time having ample coal and water capacity. A boiler pressure of 170lb/sq in gave the tractive effort of 17,000lb, with an axle load on all four coupled axles of no more than 6.6 tons. The tender had a capacity for 1500 gallons of water, and 4 tons of coal. They were distinctive in being the only tender locomotives ever to run on the narrow gauge in the British Isles, and the only ones of the 4-8-0 type.

However much the railway may have been an 'Aunt Sally' for the purveyor of railway jokes there was no lack of enterprise in the locomotive department, and in 1910 two new 4-6-2 tank engines of an enlarged and improved design were delivered from Hawthorn Leslie & Co of Newcastle. Although obviously having larger boilers and much longer side tanks there were a number of technical changes. The significant development of the type may be judged from the following table:

LLSR 4–6–2 TANKS

Locomotive Numbers	*7, 8*	*9, 10*	*13, 14*
Date	*1901*	*1904*	*1910*
Builder	*Hudswell Clark*	*Kerr Stuart*	*Hawthorn Leslie*
Total heating surface, sq ft	779.25	650	803
Grate area, sq ft	12.5	11.0	11.5
Boiler pressure, lb/sq in	150	150	175
Tank capacity, gallons	850	700	1300
Coal capacity, tons	1.25	1.0	1.75
Max axle load, tons	8.0	7.0	8.35
Tractive effort at 85% boiler pressure, lb	14,050	12,000	15,250

It is interesting that the three designs all had different types of valve gear. Nos 7 and 8 had Allan's straight link motion – the only engines in Ireland to do so – Nos 9 and 10 had Stephenson's link motion, while Nos 13 and 14 had Walschaerts radial gear.

The climax of Lough Swilly locomotive development came in 1912, when in a design specified by Ingham Sutcliffe, locomotive superintendent, and built by Hudswell Clark & Co, a machine of the same all-round capacity as the 4-8-0s but in tank engine form was produced. They were the only 4-8-4s ever to run in the British Isles, and were in many ways a remarkable design. They were given the running numbers 5 and 6 and allocated to the Letterkenny & Burtonport extension. With a tank capacity of 1500 gallons and a coal capacity of 2½ tons, these fine locomotives were capable of undertaking any duties previously handled by the 4-8-0 tender type. To increase flexibility on the many curves encountered on the line the leading coupled wheels were flangeless. They carried a boiler pressure of 180lb/sq in, and the tractive effort of 17,350lb was the highest of any Irish narrow gauge locomotive. The maximum axle load was 8.5 tons. They remained in service throughout the period covered by this book, at the end of which the steam locomotive stock of the railway stood as follows:

Locomotive Nos	Type	Builder
1–4	4–6–0T	Barclay
5–6	4–8–4T	Hudswell Clark
7–8	4–6–2T	Hudswell Clark
10	4–6–2T	Kerr Stuart
12	4–8–0	Hudswell Clark
13–14	4–6–2T	Hawthorn Leslie
15–16	4–6–2T	Hudswell Clark

By the end of the second world war, Nos 1, 7, 13 and 14 had also been scrapped, leaving 10 locomotives in service. By 1939 the service on the Burtonport extension had been reduced to one mixed train a day, leaving Londonderry at 10.00am and Burtonport at 8.30am taking 5 hours 35 minutes and 5 hours 5 minutes respectively. There was also one train in each direction between Letterkenny and Burtonport, with which there were connecting buses to and from Londonderry. The total journey times by these buses were 4½ hours down and 4 hours 10 minutes up, one hour *faster*, in each case than by train all the way! On the trains from Londonderry the locomotives worked through over the 74 miles, and together with the runs between Letterkenny and the western terminus required four locomotives in steam each day for the Burtonport line alone. The mixed trains were very heavy at times, and even in the more enlightened days of the 1930s they became very unpunctual because of the amount of shunting involved intermediately. Mr H. C. Casserley travelling by the 8.30am up from Burtonport, has recorded that with the surviving 4-8-0 No 12 they arrived at Londonderry with two passenger carriages and twenty goods wagons about $\frac{3}{4}$-hour late.

By 1890 the Belfast & Northern Counties Railway had absorbed both the Ballymena, Cushendall & Redbay Railway, and the Ballymena & Larne; but before Bowman Malcolm had begun to impress his individuality in design upon the narrow gauge section of the BNCR the two originally independent railways had managed to acquire a strange miscellany of locomotives. The BC&RR had only three locomotives of its own, all 0-4-2 saddle tanks, and as the last of these were scrapped in 1923 they hardly enter the present story. The Ballymena & Larne had six locomotives before its absorbtion by the BNCR and five of them survived to enter LMS ownership of the NCC in 1923. There were two of the very picturesque Beyer Peacock 2-4-0 side tanks, similar to those in use on the Isle of Man Railway, one of which had been scrapped in 1918. Then there were three 0-6-0 tanks, also from Beyer Peacock and dating from 1887; finally there was an isolated 2-6-0 saddle tank, built in 1880. The basic dimensions of these six locomotives were:

BNCR No	Date built	Type	Cylinders dia×stroke, in	Coupled wheel dia ft in		Overall weight tons	Tractive effort lb
105	1880	2–4–0	12½×18	3	9	19.15	7440
106	1877	0–6–0	13×18	3	9	21.05	8050
107	1877	0–6–0	13×18	3	9	21.05	8050
108	1883	0–6–0	13×18	3	9	21.05	8050
109	1880	2–6–0	14×18	3	3	25.70	10800

Of the above, No 105 was sold out of service in 1928.

Both the Cushendall line and the Ballymena & Larne included some very heavy gradients. The climb from sea level at Larne includes a fearsome initial bank of 1 in 36–44, followed by gradually easing gradients to Ballyboley Junction, whence there was a stretch of $4\frac{1}{2}$ miles continuously at 1 in 87–75 to the summit at Ballynashee, an altitude of 650ft above sea level. From this station, 12 miles from Larne Harbour, the descent to Ballymena is continuous, averaging about 1 in 100 for 12 miles. The Cushendall line was worse. In $15\frac{1}{4}$ miles from Ballymena it climbed to an altitude of no less than 1045ft at Essatathan siding in the heart of the Antrim mountains. The hardest grades were 1 in 37–39, and having passed the summit there was a precipitous descent for $1\frac{1}{4}$ miles at 1 in 40–37 to the terminus at Retreat. It served a beautiful district, with exceptionally fine mountain scenery at Parkmore, and to this station, $13\frac{1}{2}$ miles from Ballymena, a passenger service was inaugurated in 1888. To provide adequate tractive power both for this line and for the boat expresses run between Ballymena and Larne Harbour, Bowman Malcolm designed and Beyer Peacock built a remarkable class of two-cylinder compound 2-4-2 tanks, working on the Worsdell-von Borries system. The first two of these splendid little locomotives was delivered in 1892; another two were built at the Belfast Works of the NCC in 1908–9, and the final two, also from Belfast, were turned out in 1919–20.

These 2-4-2 compounds were beautifully designed. They looked slightly odd when seen from the front, with the cylinders of different sizes, but with their characteristic slow beat of only two exhausts per revolution they purred along very sweetly. They had to run, too, with the Ballymena–Larne Harbour boat expresses. These trains were booked to cover the 25 miles westbound in 60 minutes with one stop, and in 64 minutes eastbound with three stops. They were handled in the normal way of a Worsdell-von Borries compound, from a notched lever reversing gear that notched up the high- and low-pressure valves simultaneously. The cylinders were $14\frac{3}{4}$in high-pressure and 21in low-pressure, both with a stroke of 20in; the coupled wheel diameter was 3ft 9in, and the boiler pressure 160lb/sq in. The tractive effort was 13,150lb. The weight on each of the coupled axles was 10 tons, and the total weight with 570 gallons of water and 1 ton of coal was 31.85 tons. When first introduced they were painted in the 'invisible green' livery then standard on the NCC but when I first saw them they were resplendent in Midland red. One of the two original locomotives of 1892 was rebuilt in 1931 with a larger boiler, and a four-wheeled bogie replacing the pony truck at the rear end, thus becoming the only 2-4-4 ever to run in the British Isles. The cylinders and motion remained the same, but with a higher boiler pressure of 200lb/sq in, the nominal tractive effort was increased to 16,438lb. The maximum axle-load became 12 tons.

In the meantime in 1924 the NCC had taken-over the Ballycastle Railway, $16\frac{1}{4}$ miles long from Ballymoney on the main line to Londonderry. This line had been in a poor shape for some time, and in 1924 it seemed impossible to carry on. In August of that year the NCC was persuaded to take it under its wing, and traffic was resumed after being suspended for four months. There were two ancient 0-6-0 tank engines, which the NCC scrapped at once, and two 4-4-2 side tank engines built by Kitson & Co in 1908. These locomotives, which had $14\frac{1}{2}$in by 22in cylinders, coupled wheels of 3ft 7in, and carried a pressure of 165lb/sq in, had proved rather heavy for the Ballycastle line with a maximum axle load of $10\frac{3}{4}$ tons, and the NCC transferred them after alteration to the Larne line and put them on to the boat expresses. The rebuilding was necessary to enable them to conform to the more restricted loading gauge of the Ballymena and Larne section. But the passenger service on the latter line was not to last for much longer. At the beginning of 1933 there was a lengthy railway strike in Northern Ireland, and once closed the passenger service was not resumed. I saw the ex-Ballycastle 4-4-2 tanks on goods work at Larne some two years later.

After the resumption of passenger service on the Ballycastle line it was worked on the one engine in steam principle. Two of the 2-4-2 compounds were stationed at Ballycastle, and they took turns in working the entire daily service. A second locomotive was steamed only when there was enough shunting required in Ballycastle goods yard, or when an unusually heavy train required rear-end banking assistance up the initial ascent of $2\frac{1}{2}$ miles on 1 in 50–60 from Ballycastle to Capecastle. The trains were all mixed, and on occasions a train might have many extra goods wagons attached. When I travelled, however, the loads were light and a compound 2-4-2 had a mere holiday outing with two of the splendid bogie vestibuled carriages built for the boat trains of the Ballymena & Larne. They were 50ft long and 8ft 0in wide over the mouldings. Two of these, and a couple of four-wheeled covered vans was a modest task, even on a 1 in 50 gradient.

CHAPTER 10

Dublin & South Eastern

To appreciate how it came about that this smallest of the main line railways of Ireland had two terminal stations in Dublin one must go back to the very beginnings of railways in the country. In 1817 at the little town then known as Dunleary on the south side of Dublin Bay there had been completed a fine harbour, but it had not been much used until King George IV visited Ireland; he took his departure from this harbour, and suggested that it should be renamed Kingstown. At once it began to blossom as a fashionable watering place, a yachting centre and a base for the Royal Navy. Five years later the conveyance of the Irish mail by sea was taken-over by Admiralty steam packets, and Kingstown was substituted for Howth as the Irish port. It was not surprising that with the coming of railways, and with the early English lines soon flourishing, a line from Dublin to Kingstown should have been promoted. It was incorporated before the end of George IV's reign, but the six-mile railway was not opened until 17 December 1834, and then on the standard British rail-gauge of 4ft 8½in. The Dublin & Kingstown Railway, in building a short extension of 1¾ miles to Dalkey, made a trial of the atmospheric system of propulsion, which actually lasted longer than that of Brunel's ill-starred effort on the South Devon Railway.

This Kingstown and Dalkey installation was the catalyst that prompted several other extensive trials of the atmospheric system. From the moment of its opening in 1843 engineers and many pure sightseers flocked to travel on it. Brunel, Cubitt, and Vignoles were duly impressed, though a young engineering student, Ebrington by name, having obtained permission for a 'footplate' ride on the motive carriage, got more than he bargained for. Seated in the carriage, suction was duly applied, but someone had forgotten to couple the carriage to the train, and travelling 'light engine', so to speak, the carriage was whirled over the $1\frac{3}{4}$ miles to Dalkey, it is said, in $1\frac{1}{4}$ minutes – a start-to-stop average of 84mph! While the South Devon trial of the system ended ignominiously in 1848, the Kingstown and Dalkey installation struggled on until 1855. The circumstances were, however, very different from those in South Devon. In Ireland the ordinary terminus of the suburban line from Dublin was at Kingstown. There was not any question of trying to integrate atmospheric working with that of the ordinary service, though to the very end the treasurer of the Dublin & Kingstown, James Pim, remained an unshakeable enthusiast for the system. I may add that the name of Pim remained prominently associated with the line and its successors for several generations, as will be told later.

After the line from Kingstown to Dalkey had been changed over to steam locomotive haulage in 1856 the rail gauge of the parent line into Dublin was changed to the Irish standard of 5ft 3in. In the meantime a much more ambitious project had been launched in the south-east, for in 1846 a railway originally named the Waterford, Wexford, Wicklow & Dublin had obtained its Act of Incorporation. Funds did not extend to the successful financing of such an ambitious scheme, and in 1851 the undertaking was reconstructed, abandoning the lines southward from Wicklow. Furthermore, the original northern terminus was at Dundrum, three miles short of Dublin. The line as actually built at first and renamed the Dublin & Wicklow Railway was only 25 miles long. Taking an inland course and keeping well clear of the Dublin & Kingstown Railway territory, it did not reach the coast until nearing Bray. This initial stretch was opened in 1854, with access into Dublin by running powers from Dundrum over the Dublin, Dundrum & Rathfarnham Railway. The latter had no more than a single-platform station in Harcourt Street. This line was subsequently absorbed, and with extensions southward to Wexford, reached in 1872, the railway justified its extended title of the Dublin, Wicklow & Wexford, which it retained until 1906. The DW&W also obtained authority to construct a branch line along the coast northward from Bray to join-up with the Dublin & Kingstown Railway, of which the former company obtained a lease for 35 years, later extended to perpetuity.

Although the operating company which in 1906 became the

Dublin & South Eastern had what might have appeared to be the embarrassment of two parallel lines from Bray into Dublin, they were actually developed into the two busiest commuter lines in the whole of Ireland. Just before the second world war there were 53 trains down the Kingstown line going as far as Dalkey, 20 of which went on as far as Bray, while from Harcourt Street there were 20 trains serving stations to Bray, with seven intermediate stations in the $12\frac{1}{4}$ miles. There were eleven intermediate stations in the $14\frac{1}{4}$ miles from Westland Row to Bray by the coastal route. South of Bray the service became very sparse, and very slow even by Irish main line standards of the day. At the beginning of the period covered in this book the Dublin & South Eastern suffered perhaps more than any other Irish railway from incidents due to the 'Troubles', such as the reduction to little more than scrap value of no less than 16 percent of its first line passenger locomotives in collisions caused by the saboteurs. Such was the casualty rate among them that when two new main line goods locomotives from Beyer Peacock arrived in Dublin in 1922 they were not put into traffic immediately but were sent north to Belfast for safe keeping until the civil war was over!

There can be no denying that the D&SER was a very awkward system to work, both geographically and traffic-wise. There were connections with cross-channel steamers to provide for at both ends, while at the southern end the fork in the main line at Macmine Junction, 83 miles from Dublin, with the westward extension for 33 miles to Waterford on the one hand, and nearly 20 miles eastward through Wexford to Rosslare Harbour, did not make for neat and economical locomotive workings. On the central stem of the main line, between Bray and Macmine Junction, there were only three trains in each direction daily. There was the morning mail train which connected with the Irish Mail steamer from Holyhead at Kingstown, the evening express which went through to Rosslare Harbour to connect with the Great Western steamer to Fishguard, and an all-stations train leaving Dublin at 10.00am, sections from which reached Wexford at 1.35pm and Waterford at 2.45pm. The latter service, taking $4\frac{3}{4}$ hours for $116\frac{1}{4}$ miles provided no competitive facilities for the run from Dublin against those of the GS&WR, which had two trains in 3 hours 50 minutes, even though the latter involved changing into an all-stations at Maryborough, and travelling via Kilkenny. On the D&SE the morning mail and evening train to Rosslare took a little under $2\frac{1}{2}$ hours for the $69\frac{1}{2}$ miles from Bray to Macmine Junction – a not very startling average speed of $28\frac{3}{4}$mph.

Before the 'Troubles' the Dublin & South Eastern Railway had 67 locomotives, but only 50 survived to enter Great Southern Railways stock in 1925. Even though the stud had been augmented by the two new 2-6-0 main line goods locomotives in 1922 and two new 4-4-2 tanks in 1924, the D&SE could only contribute 54 locomotives to the new organisation and of these 13 were scrapped almost at once. The 41 that received GSR numbers were made up as follows:

GSR Nos	Type	GSR class	Original builder	Date
422	2-4-0	G7	Sharp Stewart	1864
423–426	2-4-0T	G1	Grand Canal St Works	1889–1895
428–433	2-4-2T	F2	Grand Canal St Works	1886–1898
434–439	2-4-2T	F1	Grand Canal St Works	1910–1909
440–449	0-6-0	J (various)	Various	1891–1910
450–453	4-4-0	D9	Vulcan Foundry	1895–1896
454	4-4-0	D8	Beyer Peacock	1905
455–457	4-4-2T	C2	Grand Canal Street and Beyer Peacock	1911 and 1924
458–460	4-4-2T	C3	Sharp Stewart	1893
461–2	2-6-0	K2	Beyer Peacock	1922

There was one other 2-4-2 tank engine not specified in the foregoing list, No 427, which had a curious origin and a momentous subsequent career. It was in 1902, when the Dublin Wickow & Wexford Railway was short of locomotives, that arrangements were made to purchase six of the LNWR 4ft 6in 2-4-2 tanks of a design introduced by F. W. Webb in 1879, of which no fewer than 180 were built at Crewe. The class came to include also 40 earlier locomotives of a 2-4-0 type, which were converted into 2-4-2Ts. The rebuilding work to make them suitable for 5ft 3in gauge was carried out at Crewe, where also they were painted in the then standard green of the DW&WR. The one that became No 427 of the GSR was actually an earlier conversion, because it had started life as a 2-4-0 tank engine built at Crewe in 1877. In common with DW&WR passenger locomotives the six arrivals from the LNWR were named, in this case after earls. No 64, the one that became GSR No 427, was *Earl of Bessborough*, while the other five were: 59 *Earl Fitzwilliam*, 60 *Earl of Courtown*, 61 *Earl of Wicklow*, 62 *Earl of Meath*, and 63 *Earl of Carysfort*. Apart from the colour and the method of displaying their names they arrived in Ireland looking every inch London & North Western Railway locomotives.

They were put onto the Dublin—Bray passenger service but from all accounts did not prove very popular, and when the war came five were sold to the British Government and re-converted to 4ft 8½in gauge, three during 1916 and two in 1917. No 64 remained in Ireland, and in 1922 was encased in armour-plate, and used to haul an armoured train during the 'Troubles'. The odd thing about this was that although the Dublin & South Eastern Railway became desperately short of motive power at that time, No 64 thus encased was transferred to the Great Southern & Western Railway, and was for a time stationed in County Kerry. After the end of the civil war, and stripped of the armour it survived in ordinary service as GSR No 427 until 1936.

Having become thus involved through No 427 with the stud of 2-4-2 tank engines, it will be convenient to continue with an account of the indigenous F1 and F2 classes, the six locomotives each of which were all built at the Grand Canal Street Works, on the Dublin and Kingstown line. Building, however, consisted of little more than assembly. The works was small and cramped, with little in the way of general mechanical engineering facilities. There was no boiler shop as such, so that boilers and their mountings were usually purchased complete from one or another of the English manufacturers. The DW&W had done well in 1897 to secure the services of Richard Cronin as locomotive superintendent, because he had been works manager at Inchicore, where design and workshop practice were second to none at that time, if not on the same scale as that of the great English works. It was at this time also that the practice of naming locomotives began, the selection of titles being made by Miss Ida Pim, a niece of the Chairman of the company, Frederick W. Pim. More recent instances of ladies choosing titles for locomotives that may be recalled were those of Mrs C. B.

Collett selecting names for some of the Great Western express locomotives in Churchward's day, and of Mrs Violet Godfrey, daughter of Sir Nigel Gresley choosing names for some of the famous A4 streamlined Pacifics of the LNER.

Ida Pim had an almost obvious choice for the first new locomotive turned out by Richard Cronin, for the 2-4-2 tank No 3 was completed on St Patrick's day 1898. Naturally it was named *St Patrick*, and the five subsequent locomotives of the class that became GSR F2 were made by conversions from William Wakefield's 2-4-0 tanks that dated from 1884. There had been twelve of this class, and the five that were converted to 2-4-2s were:

D&SER No	Name	Originally built	Date converted	GSR No
10	*St Senanus*	1896	1903	429*
11	*St Kevin*	1896	1900	430
28	*St Lawrence*	1887	1909	431
45	*St Keiran*	1886	1910	432
46	*Princess Mary*	1888	1911	433

*This locomotive was scrapped in 1925 and never actually bore its allotted GSR number.

Of the remaining seven of Wakefield's 1884 class of 2-4-0 tanks, four entered GSR service as Nos 423–6, and their previous history was thus:

No. DW&W D&SER	Name	Built	Withdrawn	GSR No
49	*Carrickmines*	1891	1955	423
9	*Dalkey*	1890	1952	424
47	*Stillorgan*	1889	1953	425
7	—	1895	1926	426
1	—	1892	1925	—
2	*Glenageary*	1885	1925	—
6	—	1894	1925	—

As originally built the 2-4-0 tanks had 16in by 24in cylinders, but both those that remained as 2-4-0s and those converted to 2-4-2 were enlarged subsequently to 17in by 24in. The coupled wheels were 5ft 6in diameter, and the boiler pressure 150lb/sq in. Except for No 429, the five remaining 2-4-2 tanks of Class F2 were not scrapped until 1950–1957.

The success of Cronin's first 2-4-2 tanks led to the construction of six more being authorised, but because of the conditions prevailing at Grand Canal Street works the completion of these locomotives was spread over eight years. They were none-the-less excellent for that, and survived all the vicissitudes of the years that followed to live on into a great age. The earliest to be scrapped went in 1950. Their names, numbers and building dates were:

DSER No	Name	Date built	GSR No	Date withdrawn
12	St Brigid	1901	435	1950
48	St Selskar	1902	439	1952
8	St Brendan	1903	434	1950
29	St Mantan	1906	437	1951
27	St Aidan	1907	436	1953
30	St Iberius	1909	438	1952

They were classed F1 by the GSR, and like F2 they had 17in by 24in cylinders, 5ft 6in coupled wheels, but carried a higher boiler pressure of 160lb/sq in. Their tanks carried 1500 gallons of water, and the bunkers 2½ tons of coal.

The 12 2-4-2 tank engines bore the brunt of the busy passenger workings on both routes between Dublin and Bray. It was not only on the local trains. Tank engines worked the through trains to the south as far as Bray, where they were changed for tender 2-4-0s or 4-4-0s. But in the Dublin area where most of the profitable business of the Dublin & South Eastern Railway lay the workings were complex, to say the least of it. This arose from the injection of the mail and boat trains services into a busy commuter run at Dun Laoghaire, as Kingstown became after the establishment of the Irish Free State. Furthermore, in the 1930s the closing of the Broadstone terminus of the former Midland Great Western Railway and the bringing of the main line trains from Galway and Sligo into Westland Row brought periods of intense working into that none-too-commodious station. The trouble was that it had long ceased to be a terminus. For that the mail traffic and the English connections were responsible. From an early date in the history of railway communication the mails from England to the greater part of what is now the Irish Free State have been funnelled through that brief but vital bottleneck between Dun Laoghaire and Westland Row, but to avoid road cartage across Dublin connection was desirable to the other three main line railways.

So, in 1884, the City of Dublin Junction Railway had been promoted, to connect the Dublin, Wicklow & Wexford with the other three railways via Amiens Street. It was an expensive short link, most of it on viaduct, including the crossing of the River Liffey; junction with the Great Northern was made at Amiens Street itself, with the MGW at Newcomen Bridge Junction and with the GS&W in a link just north of Amiens Street by a short line leading to North Strand Road Junction, on the line down to the terminus at North Wall. This new connecting line from Westland Row, in which the Great Northern and the City of Dublin Steam Packet Company were joint sponsors with the DW&W, was opened in 1891. The steam packet company then had the Post Office contract for conveyance of the Irish Mail by sea between Kingstown and Holyhead, and so was initially involved. The short link between the GS&W line at North Strand Junction and Amiens Street was not opened until 1895, and mail trains to and from Kingstown were worked over a connecting line between the GS&W and MGW lines at Glasnevin Junction and brought onto the new City of Dublin Junction line at Newcomen Bridge Junction. Mails from Cork thus passed successively over the GS&W, MGW, City of Dublin Junction, and the DW&W before reaching the mail steamer.

The line had not long been open before an arrangement was made between the GS&W and the DW&W for the latter company to work the mail trains throughout from Kingstown Pier through the centre of Dublin onto the MGW line at Newcomen Bridge Junction, thence over Glasnevin Junction and the western GS&W loop to the Cork main line at Island Bridge Junction. It was a sharply-curved line which included a 1 in 60 bank between Amiens Street and Newcomen Bridge. Mainly to provide for the working of the mail trains over this awkward link, the DW&W in 1893 purchased three handsome 4-4-2 tank engines from Sharp Stewart & Co. They were by some way the most powerful locomotives that the DW&W had so far possessed, having 18in by 26in cylinders, 5ft 3in coupled wheels, and boiler pressure of 150lb/sq in. These locomotives, smartly styled, were at first unnamed, but around 1905 they were named as follows:

DW&W		GSR
No	Name	No
52	*Duke of Connaught*	458
53	*Duke of Abercorn*	459
54	*Duke of Leinster*	460

They were not scrapped until the 1950s.

The construction of the City of Dublin Junction involved the complete remodelling of Westland Row station. Hitherto, in rather cramped circumstances, it had coped with the suburban service to Kingstown and Bray, and one long-distance passenger train a day in each direction, connecting with the night mails to and from Holyhead. To provide for the trains on the City of Dublin Junction line two through platforms were provided, and three bay platforms for trains from the Kingstown direction terminating and leaving. Before the first world war there were three services from Kingstown to Holyhead, there being a midday express connecting with an LNWR steamer, in addition to the day and night mails; there were often two boat trains for each service, because so many through carriages were provided to bring long-distance passengers alongside the steamers. The boat train operation, worked exclusively either by 2-4-2, or one of the three 4-4-2 tank engines, was extremely smart, and the second boat train in connection with the up night mail was advertised to arrive on the pier only three minutes before the departure time of the steamer!

In the morning the night Irish Mail steamer was due to arrive at Kingstown at 5.30am, and the one connecting train booked to leave at 5.37am was a heavy one because it conveyed not only through carriages for Cork, and Belfast, but also the GS&W and GN breakfast cars, that would be going through on the respective mail trains. There were also MGW coaches for Broadstone; travelling on these latter, however, passengers had to change into the 'Limited Mail' for the westward journey. With no more than the 12 2-4-2 tanks, three 4-4-2s, aided by the seven little 2-4-0 tanks, the locomotive utilisation must have been very high, because those 22 tank engines had to handle not only the many commuter trains, but the mails between Kingstown and Westland Row, and also the main line trains to the south, all of which changed locomotives at Bray. The stud, which was completed by the construction of the last 2-4-2 tank in 1909, was augmented in 1911 by the addition of one new locomotive, an enlarged 4-4-2 tank No 20, and named appropriately for that year *King George*. The cylinders were 18in by 26in, coupled wheels 6ft 0in diameter, and the boiler pressure 175lb/sq in. The tanks had a capacity of 1700 gallons, and the bunker for three tons of coal. Certain commentators have remarked that this fine-looking locomotive proved none too successful, but when additional locomotives were required in 1924 (even though a different locomotive superintendent was in charge) two more units were obtained from Beyer Peacock & Co, identical to No 20 except for having Belpaire fireboxes. All three survived the *second* world war.

The end of the civil war left the Dublin & South Eastern with no more than five main line 4-4-0 passenger locomotives in serviceable condition, and only two of the former 'Mail' 2-4-0s. The casualties had been the 4-4-0 express No 68 *Rathcoole*, and the 2-4-0 No 25, formerly *Glenart*. Of the 2-4-0s No 26 had earlier been converted to a tank engine and worked on the Shillelagh branch. The 4-4-0s were of two classes. The first, consisting of four numbered 55 to 58 did not get off to a very good start from all accounts. They were ordered from the Vulcan Foundry in the 3-year gap between the superintendencies of W. Wakefield and Richard Cronin — 1894 to 1897 — when the locomotive department was under the management of the civil engineer. He appears to have been dogmatic over the specification for these locomotives, beyond his appreciation of the factors involved. The little 2-4-0 'Mail' locomotives had cylinders 16in by 22in. The civil engineer in contact with the Vulcan foundry had recommended to him a design of 4-4-0 having 17in diameter cylinders, but apparently at his insistence the cylinders were made 18in by 26in and the locomotives did not steam well. This deficiency was blamed on the small boilers originally fitted when the locomotives were supplied from England in 1895, but I do not think the trouble can be blamed on the size of the boiler. In 1906 Cronin fitted an entirely new boiler to No 57, which wrought a positive transformation in performance, yet the only outward difference was the use of a Belpaire firebox. The respective heating surfaces were as shown in the following table. It is more than likely that the draughting was at fault on the original locomotives, and that Cronin, as an experienced locomotive engineer, put his finger on the trouble.

DW&Wk 4–4–0 BOILERS

Details	Original 1895	New, Belpaire 1906
Heating surface, sq ft		
Tubes	935.4	993
Firebox	91.5	101
Grate area, sq ft	19.68	18.5
Boiler pressure, lb/sq in	150	160

The remaining three locomotives were subsequently altered to agree with No 57, and in that form lasted for many years. At the time of Cronin's arrival from Inchicore they were named thus:

DW&W (AND D&SE) 4–4–0s

Original No	Name	GSR No	Date withdrawn
55	Rathdown	450	1929
56	Rathmines	451	1934
57	Rathnew	452	1933
58	Rathdrum	453	1940

The last to survive had a second rebuild in 1915, receiving a considerably larger boiler with a combined total heating surface of 1149sq ft, but the elegant appearance of the locomotive was largely destroyed. The longevity of most of them was partly explained by all except No 55 receiving new frames.

Cronin's own 4-4-0s, Nos 67 *Rathmore* and 68 *Rathcoole*, were purchased from Beyer Peacock & Co in 1905 for use on the mail trains between Bray and Wexford. Like their predecessors they had 18in by 26in cylinders, 6ft 0in coupled wheels, but a larger boiler having a combined heating surface of 1193sq ft and carrying a pressure of 175lb/sq in. They were distinctive in having their names incorporated in the traditional Beyer

Peacock brass splasher beading, in contrast to names painted in large letters on the splashers or on the side tanks. In 1923 No 68 was damaged beyond repair in a collision with former 'Mail' 2-4-0 No 25 near Waterford, because of activities during the Civil War. The 2-4-0 was also a write-off as a result. But No 67, which became GSR No 454 in 1925, lasted until 1949.

When Cronin retired in 1917 he was succeeded by G. F. Wild, who will be remembered by his massive 2-6-0s, built by Beyer Peacock & Co in 1922 for working the night goods trains between Dublin and Wexford. They had 19in by 26in cylinders, 5ft 1in coupled wheels, and a large boiler including a superheater, for the first time on the D&SER. The combined total heating surface was 1248sq ft and the grate area 20sq ft. The boiler pressure was 175lb/sq in. The tenders carried 2600 gallons of water and five tons of coal. Although there was a great infusion of locomotives of non-D&SER origin after the amalgamation of 1925, the two 2-6-0s Nos 15 and 16 which became GSR Nos 461–2, remained on the job for which they were designed and lasted out steam on the line. No 462 was withdrawn in 1963 after more than 40 years, and it is good to know that No 461 which had a working life of 43 years is preserved.

All in all, the Dublin & South Eastern was a busy and efficiently-run railway. I have many memories of its most intensively-worked section from Dun Laoghaire into Dublin, though I must admit the mind is not at its most receptive at 6.00am after a night crossing from Holyhead, especially on arrival at the pier before dawn on a chilly winter morning; the short run up to Dublin gave just enough time to get into overalls ready to ride on the footplate down to Cork, or up to Belfast. In

Plate 13(a) Ex-GS&WR 4–4–0 No 95, of J. A. F. Aspinall's elegant mail locomotives of 1885; this photograph shows it as fitted with the later type of two-ring boiler. This locomotive remained in service until 1955. (*L&GRP*)
(b) Ex-MGW 2–4–0 No 662 rebuilt with large boiler, superheater and Belpaire firebox. Originally No 21 *Swift*, it was built 1896, and scrapped 1955. (*L&GRP*)
(c) Ex-GS&WR 4–4–0 No 331, built at Inchicore in 1906 by R. Coey, here seen in final form with superheated boiler and Belpaire firebox; scrapped 1959. (*L&GRP*)

Plate 14(a) GNR(I): Glover three-cylinder compound 4—4—0 No 83 *Eagle*, in the blue livery. (*L&GRP*)

(b) GNR(I): No 173 *Galteemore*, first of the new 4—4—0s of 1938 replacing the older Glover 4—4—0s of the same names and numbers, with deeper frames, improved valve gear, and painted blue. (*O. S. Nock*)

the 1930s the connection to the main line mail trains, leaving the pier at 6.10am was not advertised in the ordinary commuter timetable between Dun Laoghaire and Westland Row. The first train of the day was the 6.30am 'Boat Express', non-stop to Westland Row purely for Dublin passengers. It was pleasant to arrive from England by the day mail and instead of going on to Dublin immediately on the 5.40pm boat express to pause awhile and watch the trains: see the 5.55pm, 6.13pm, 6.25pm, 6.43pm, 6.57pm leave for Dublin, and the 5.50pm, 6.02pm, 6.22pm, 6.30pm, 6.37pm and 6.50pm come down, all of them hauled by tank engines — then perhaps travel up to Dublin on the Waterford Mail, which called at Dun Laoghaire at 7.25pm and ran thence non-stop to Westland Row. Of the complications that developed at the latter station consequent upon the closing of the former MGWR terminus of Broadstone I must keep until the next chapter.

CHAPTER 11

Rationalisation on the GSR

When the Great Southern Railways was formed in 1925 following the passing of the Railways Act of 1924, the new company possessed 587 locomotives, contained however in no fewer than 114 classes. Of these totals the GS&WR and the MGW contributed 473, in 61 classes, leaving 114 locomotives of 53 different classes remaining. To anyone having ideas of general standardisation it could have been a staggering prospect. Without knowing anything of the prevailing context one could have decreed, for a start, scrap those 114 outright and replace them with one or two new standard modern types. But finance was just not available for a comprehensive policy of scrap and build. Eire was only just recovering from civil war, and quite apart from any financial considerations the once-warring factions had to be gradually brought together again. I was never more conscious of the sociological factors than on one of my earliest footplate journeys between Dublin and Cork. We had the same locomotive in both directions, but it was whispered to me that the two drivers I had ridden with had been on opposite sides in the civil war!

In this very difficult time of consolidation the locomotive department of the GSR was fortunate in having at its head men of the engineering ability and warm human outlook, such as J. R. Bazin, the Chief Mechanical Engineer, and his deputy and eventual successor, W. H. Morton. How the pair of them, both themselves Englishmen, must have looked wistfully across the Irish Sea to the standardisation projects being developed on the British railways following Grouping, though a mild stroke of luck had come Morton's way just before the Midland Great Western Railway lost its separate identity. Just after the Armistice of 1918, to avoid Woolwich Arsenal being thrown into virtual idleness by the sudden end of the need for munitions Winston Churchill, then Minister of Munitions, had conceived the idea of turning that great plant over to locomotive production to help make up the arrears of new production that had been forced upon the British railway works by the war. But there had been much argument among locomotive engineers in England as to what types should be ordered. No one of the British railways was keen on having locomotives built by a plant with no previous experience, and in the end R. E. L. Maunsell who had been Chief Mechanical Engineer to the Railway Executive Committee during the war, somewhat reluctantly agreed to 100 of his SECR N Class 2-6-0s being built.

In the mood of independence and individuality following the end of the war he was fairly sure no one else would want them. And so it turned out, and the Government was left with 100 locomotives on its hands. Almost as a measure of despair a few of the finished locomotives were sent to Ashford as samples. As expected, because of the lack of experience with locomotive work at Woolwich each one had to be thoroughly vetted before going into service, and it was only as a result of a bargain offer at a greatly reduced price that the Southern Railway agreed to take 50, which were constantly in trouble until they had received their first general repair. On the Midland Great Western Morton arranged for the purchase of 12 complete sets of parts for these locomotives, to be erected at Broadstone, and in the process converted to the 5ft 3in gauge. With careful and expert erection they proved successful, and a further 15 were subsequently purchased by the GSR. These locomotives were the only substantial addition to stock that the GSR received in the first 15 years of its existence, and they allowed a limited number of earlier and already obsolete units to be scrapped. Otherwise, until the three beautiful Queens appeared in 1939 it was largely a case of 'make-do-and-mend'.

As this chapter has opened with some reference to the origin of the 'Woolworths', as they were nicknamed (more correctly GSR Class K1) the details of design as adapted to Irish conditions may be quoted. The official photograph showed the first as No 410, but it actually went into traffic on the MGW section as No 372.

CLASS K1 2–6–0 LOCOMOTIVES

Cylinders	19in by 28in
Coupled wheels	5ft 6in
Boiler pressure	200 lb/sq in
Heating surface:	
Tubes	1391 sq ft
Firebox	135 sq ft
Superheater (21 elements)	285 sq ft
Total	1811 sq ft
Grate area	25 sq ft
Adhesion weight	47.9 tons
Total locomotive weight	61 tons
Tender:	
Water capacity	3500 gallons
Coal	5 tons
Loaded weight	39.25 tons
Locomotive and tender weight	100.25 tons
Tractive effort at 85% boiler pressure	26,000 lb

The new locomotives were thus the most powerful in Ireland, surpassing Mr Bazin's 500 Class mixed-traffic 4-6-0s on the former GSWR, which had a tractive effort of 23,780lb. But the 'Woolworths' came into service slowly: two in 1925, eight in 1926, five in 1927, three in 1928, two in 1929, and six in 1930. This last batch had 6ft 0in coupled wheels instead of 5ft 6in. The numbers ran from 372 to 398, but the set of parts allocated to No 392 was never assembled, but kept as spares. It may be added that Morton secured purchase of these sets from the British Government at a price of £2,000 each – a bargain even for those days!

Two engines of Mr Bazin's mixed-traffic 4-6-0 class, Nos 501 and 502, were built at Inchicore in 1926, and in 1928 the prototype for what was intended to be a general replacement for the ageing stud of suburban tank engines on the Dublin & South Eastern, and also as initially stated, for the Cork, Bandon & South Coast line. But this handsome 2-6-2 tank, with outside cylinders and Walschaerts valve gear, No 850, proved to be the only one of its kind, for shortly after it went into traffic the depression struck hard, and no new construction was undertaken for a few years. No 850 had 17½in by 28in cylinders, 5ft 6in coupled wheels, a total heating surface, including superheater, of 1056sq ft and worked at a pressure of 160lb/sq in. As compared to the largest of the Dublin & South Eastern tank engines, Wild's 4-4-2s of 1924, the tractive effort of 16,000lb was *less*, against the 17,175lb of the 4-4-2.

The Cork, Bandon & South Coast Railway was the smallest of the four involved in the amalgamation of 1925, having a route mileage of only 66, and only 20 locomotives to be taken into the GSR, but eight of these were very useful 4-6-0 tank engines, first introduced in 1906. Like many Irish locomotive classes their introduction was gradual, one locomotive being added in each of the years 1909, 1910, 1912, 1914 and 1919, with a final two in 1920. They had 18in by 24in cylinders, 5ft 2½in coupled wheels, and carried a boiler pressure of 160lb/sq in. The water capacity of the tanks was 1100 gallons, and the coal bunker took 2¾ tons, adequate for the run from Cork to Baltimore, 61¾ miles. In view of the initial suggestion that locomotives of the Bazin 2-6-2 tank type might be put on to this route it is interesting that the tractive effort of the 'native' 4-6-0 tanks was 15,200lb. In the event all survived the second world war, and the last was not scrapped until 1965. One, at least, was tried in the Dublin commuter service of the D&SER section, and I should imagine did very well.

One of the most urgent and immediate concerns of the locomotive department of the GSR was to bring relief to the hard-pressed men and machines of the former Dublin & South Eastern line. Because of the hazardous conditions of the time of the civil war locomotives had been kept in traffic far beyond their normal span between visits to shops for overhaul. The works at Grand Canal Street, even in ordinary circumstances was frequently working on a shoestring; in such untoward conditions as prevailed from 1921 onwards, repairs were often a case of just patching-up and hoping for the best. Over the rest of the GSR system business was at a low ebb, in the aftermath of the 'Troubles', but neither the GS&W nor the MGW had been affected to anything like the same extent as had the D&SER relative to its total locomotive stock; the immediate task was to send such locomotives as could be spared to help out. The Irish enthusiasts who sent details of their observations to *The Railway Magazine* had a tremendously interesting time from the very beginning of 1925; but there was much curiosity as to how the visiting locomotives were doing, for the circumstances were very different from those of a definite locomotive interchange trial. It was a rescue operation in which any locomotive in reasonably good condition and acceptable to the civil engineer was more than welcome.

Fortunately from the locomotive point of view the loads were not heavy, nor the schedules demanding, and the vintage 2-4-0s and 0-6-0s that were transferred from the Midland Great Western section were able to cope well enough. The infusion of these, plus some of much the same vintage from the GS&WR section enabled proper works attention to be given to the former D&SER locomotives, and many were sent either to Broadstone or Inchicore for heavy general repairs. Some concern, however, was felt among outside observers when the two relatively new 2-6-0s Nos 15 and 16 were taken off the night Dublin–Wexford goods, and replaced on the job by two former GS&W 0-6-0s of roughly equal tractive power. These two, Nos 249 and 252, were of the last batch of non-superheater locomotives before the introduction of R. E. L. Maunsell's superheated version in 1913. They had the same cylinder and coupled wheel dimensions, and carried the same boiler pressure. The transfer of the GS&WR 0-6-0s proved no more than temporary, and Wild's fine 2-6-0s returned to the job for which they were designed, remaining on it except for occasional visits to works until the end of steam traction.

A feature of the amalgamation which soon became apparent was the removal of locomotive names. Wild had dispensed with the names on most of the D&SER passenger locomotives, but on the MGWR nearly everything was named. A dark grey devoid of any lining-out became the standard painting style, with numberplates like those of the former GS&WR. The Inchicore locomotives retained their former numbers, which ran from 1 to 371, 400 to 409, and 500 to 502, while separated from all the rest were the two 4-8-0 shunting tanks of Watson's design, Nos 900 and 901. The Woolwich 2-6-0s were numbered 372 to 391 (with the 5ft 6in driving wheels) and 393 to 398 (with 6ft driving wheels). The former D&SER stock began at 422. After the merger, the allocations in 1925 were thus:

Dublin & South Eastern	422–462
Cork, Bandon & South Coast	463–482
Waterford & Tramore	483–486
Cork & Macroom Direct	487–491
ex-Allman's Distillery	495
Midland Great Western	530–668

A number of the older locomotives included in the above never carried their allocated GSR numbers, but were scrapped soon after the amalgamation.

To English enthusiasts of an earlier generation the name of Alexander McDonnell will be associated with an unhappy time on the North Eastern Railway when a man from Ireland was appointed to succeed that veritable patriarch of locomotive superintendents, Edward Fletcher, at Gateshead. The newcomer, horrified at the total and bewildering lack of standardisation among North Eastern locomotives set to work to change all that. Now the railway Geordies of the 1880s may have been radical enough when it came to British politics, but where locomotives were concerned they were about the most diehard lot of conservatives that could be imagined, and utterly devoted to Fletcher and all his works. So when this man from Ireland arrived and started to change everything, it was not long before North Eastern England was seething with indignation and fury. In a matter of months the enginemen had virtually forced his resignation! It was an extraordinary sequel to what had been a remarkably successful tenure of office at Inchicore that had lasted for 19 years, and left the GS&WR with well over a hundred locomotives that not only passed into GSR ownership in 1925, but with diligent repair work lasted until they were nearly 100 years old! Construction of his standard 0-6-0 goods locomotive first introduced in 1867 was continued by three very distinguished successors at Inchicore, J. A. F. Aspinall, H. A. Ivatt and Robert Coey, until no fewer than 111 were in service. The entire stud came into GSR ownership in 1925, only 12 failing to survive to the end of the period of this book, and the majority lasted into the 1960s.

Of course one can appreciate that not a great deal of the originals would be left when one of the earliest, No 150, built in 1867, lasted for 90 years; No 151, built in 1868, surpassed even this by not being withdrawn until 1965. Many of them were rebuilt with larger boilers and Belpaire fireboxes, but when I was at Cork in 1937 and again in 1939 I saw a number with the original size boilers, though these had the later type with a two-ring barrel, and the dome set a little farther to the rear than on the McDonnell originals, which had a three-ring barrel. One cannot fail to be struck by the remarkable likeness of these locomotives to John Ramsbottom's DX Class express goods 0-6-0s on the London & North Western Railway. As a young graduate of Dublin University, McDonnell had been appointed locomotive superintendent of the Newport, Abergavenny & Hereford Railway, and had then come into contact with the practice of Crewe Works; as a consequence he had become a great admirer of John Ramsbottom. Not only was his 101 Class 0-6-0 very similar to the DX, but his first express passenger 2-4-0 was even more recognisable as an Irish version of the Crewe Newton Class. The 101 Class originally had 17in by 24in cylinders, 5ft 2in coupled wheels and carried a pressure of 140lb/sq in. It was only in this latter that they differed from the DX, which had only 120lb/sq in. The 101 Class later had 18in cylinders, and the boilers had the standard 160lb/sq in pressure used on the GS&WR.

None of the McDonnell main line express 2-4-0s survived to enter GSR ownership, though of the Aspinall version that followed in 1883, was virtually the same except for use of a leading bogie; at least No 54 dating from 1883 survived until 1959. Of these locomotives the larger variety of Aspinall 4-4-0 introduced in 1885, a total of 35 entered GSR stock in 1925. By that time they had received two-ring boilers; many of them retained the raised firebox casings as a relic of McDonnells practice and the double folding pattern of smokebox doors which met in a vertical joint on the centre line. There were many of these smokebox doors still to be seen on the former GS&W system in the later 1930s. The Aspinall 4-4-0s had a striding elegance about their appearance which I found most attractive. The McDonnell 0-6-0s, which were fitted with larger boilers having Belpaire fireboxes, lost something of their original grace, but it speaks volumes for the frame design that it could sustain the considerably higher tractive power it was required to transmit in these later years.

Another remarkable case of rebuilding was that of the

Midland Great Western 5ft 8in 2-4-0s of 1893–8, (GSR Class G2) with new superheated boilers. Morton had superheated them from 1917 onwards, retaining flat slide-valves, but since 1930 a number of them were fitted with the standard Inchicore Class Y boiler. This had the following dimensions: tubes 673 sq ft, firebox 98sq ft, and superheater 112sq ft. The grate area was 15.5sq ft and the pressure 150lb/sq in. As rebuilt a second time these locomotives had a massive rather 'over ripe' appearance, which the setting of the chimney rather forward on the smokebox seemed to accentuate. They were noteworthy in being the only superheated 2-4-0s in existence; as such their lives were very much prolonged and although originating as far back as 1893–8 none of them was withdrawn before 1954, while the longest lived lasted until 1963. This was No 653, originally MGWR No 19 *Spencer*, built at Broadstone in 1894. A number were transferred to Bray shed for working on the D&SE lines, both to Harcourt Street and to Westland Row, where they were joined by a few of the Aspinall 4-4-0s from the GS&W section.

The rebuilding of the various batches of the Coey express 4-4-0s also involved various stages, some of which were due to E. A. Watson. At the time the GSR was formed they were grouped as follows:

GSR Class	Running numbers	First introduced
D11	301 to 304	1900
D12	305 to 308	1902
D10	309 to 314	1903
D2	321 to 332	1904

The rebuilding, or virtual renewal of No 331 by Watson, with new frames $1\frac{1}{8}$ thick instead of the original 1in, had been followed by similar renewal of Nos 327, 328, 329, 330 and 332; while a similar renewal, but with a parallel boiler, applied to Nos 321, 322 and 323. In the time when Morton was Chief Mechanical Engineer of the GSR what was known as the type O superheated boiler was fitted to Nos 327–331, which retained their original motion, while No 332 had the same standard boiler, but with piston instead of slide valves on the cylinders. Eventually all the Coey 4-4-0s looked alike but there were two different boilers, the O and the N. Their details were as follows:

Boiler class	N	O
Heating surfaces, sq ft:		
tubes	708	1084
firebox	120	136.7
superheater	168	224
Boiler pressure, lb/sq in	160	180

The N type was fitted to the 301–4 and 309–14 series, and the O to the 305–8, series, and from 321 onwards. Nos 324–326 had been scrapped in 1927–8, and by 1937 it was only No 322 that remained in its saturated condition. I saw Nos 303 and 305, working from Cork in the later 1930s.

Coey built some smaller wheeled 4-4-0s similar to the 305 series but with 5ft 7in coupled wheels, for the Cork–Rosslare boat trains, which were numbered 333 to 339. They were rebuilt in a similar way to the 6ft 7in main line express locomotives, and in 1927 No 334 was transferred to Bray shed for working the Waterford mails on the D&SE section. At that time a second ex-GSWR 4-4-0, No 302, was stationed at Bray, and these shared with the D&SE 4-4-0s Nos 57 and 57 (GSR Nos 450 and 452) the passenger workings to Wexford and Waterford. So far as transfer of locomotives was concerned, the Sunday excursion traffic from Westland Row to the coastal resorts served by the former D&SER was such that during the season 0-6-0 goods locomotives from both Inchicore and Broadstone were sent round to Westland Row to help with this. In the early days of the merger there had been numerous temporary transfers to the D&SER section, while the arrears of maintenance work on the indigenous classes was being made up. The Dublin & South Eastern locomotives in themselves were excellent, but the conditions in which they had to work during the 'Troubles' were more than locomotive 'flesh and blood' could reasonably stand.

One of the former GS&WR 4-4-0s that was stationed at Bray for some time, and usually working the Waterford mail was No 334. The successful running of this locomotive was partly the reason for the multiplication of the design in 1936, though with modifications to suit lines where the axle loading was limited. The boiler was changed to provide for a higher degree of superheat, because in the combined heating surface of 1254sq ft the superheater provided 329.7sq ft. The grate area was 20sq ft.

With 18in by 26in cylinders, coupled wheels of 5ft 8½in, and a boiler pressure of 180lb/sq in, the tractive effort was 18,800lb. One can infer, nevertheless, that this nominal figure was more than the boiler capacity could supply, because two of the five locomotives of the class had their cylinders lined up to 17in diameter, while the other three had their boiler pressure reduced to 160lb/sq in.

In view of the increasing age of the tank engines engaged in the Dublin suburban service it was natural to expect some additions to the stock, as traffic was increasing in the 1930s. While Bazin's prototype 2-6-2T No 850 had apparently been very successful it was evident that a simpler design was favoured, and in 1933 a class of five 0-6-2 tank engines was built at Inchicore. They were of very neat, simple, and compact appearance, and of no more than moderate capacity. The cylinders were 18in by 24in, the coupled wheels 5ft 6in, and the boiler pressure 160lb/sq in, providing a tractive effort of 16,020lb. The boilers were relatively small, having heating surfaces: tubes 662sq ft, firebox 112sq ft, superheater 112sq ft. The grate area was 18sq ft. The adhesion weight was only 45¼ tons and the total weight with 1500 gallons of water and 3 tons of coal, 57.35 tons. For the first time on the GSR the numbers were displayed in huge white figures on the tank sides, instead of the cast white-metal number plates so long traditional at Inchicore. They were followed in 1934 by a tender version: an 0-6-0 goods locomotive engine with boiler, cylinders and motion the same as the 0-6-2 tanks but with coupled wheels 5ft 1¾in. The tractive effort was thus proportionately higher.

Rationalisation of traffic facilities is always quoted as a point in favour of railway amalgamation, particularly in a city like Dublin where the activities of the pre-grouping companies had led to much duplication. One had only to look at two closely parallel lines running from the maze of junctions north-west of Amiens Street, out towards the west beside the Royal Canal, and four parallel lines running down to the quayside at North Wall, to realise that some rationalisation was overdue. Furthermore the Great Southern as constituted in 1925 had no fewer than *four* terminal stations in Dublin. While the justification for the Dublin & South Eastern at both Harcourt Street and Westland Row was provided amply by the intensity of the suburban service operated profitably from both stations, a big question mark hung over Broadstone. The Midland Great Western, even in its palmiest days never had any suburban traffic worth mentioning, and once the handsome station buildings had ceased to be a railway headquarters the justification for keeping such fine premises became very much less. Furthermore, the Dublin goods depot of the MGW was on the quayside at North Wall. Only the extensive cattle traffic was dealt with in a depot alongside Broadstone.

But if Broadstone were to be closed, where could the prestigious, if not very fast trains to Galway, Sligo & Westport be accommodated? To take them into Kingsbridge would involve reversal at Glasnevin and Island Bridge Junctions, while to bring them into Westland Row would mean injecting them into the busiest station in all Dublin, and taking them over the City of Dublin Junction Railway of which, even after 1925, the Great Southern owned no more than a one-third share. Quite apart from traffic or financial considerations, the direct route from the MGW line to Westland Row involved crossing the Royal Canal, near Newcomen Bridge Junction, and the lifting bridge there was barred to heavy main line locomotives. Unless the inconvenience and delay of changing from small to large locomotives on the outskirts of the city was to be incurred, it was desirable that the through locomotives should work the MGW section expresses into and out of Westland Row, and in the 1930s that meant the 'Woolworths', with their maximum axle-load of $18\frac{1}{4}$ tons.

To appreciate the situation so far as the complex of running lines is concerned one can refer to the map on page 50. The route for mail traffic to and from the former Great Southern & Western had originally been taken via the short connecting line between the Drumcondra and Glasnevin Junctions, onto the MGW line to Newcomen Bridge Junction. This was the time, as previously referred to, when the Dublin & South Eastern locomotives worked the GS&WR mail trains right through from Westland Row to Island Bridge Junction. The final link in the complex shown on the map came in 1905 when the GS&WR line from North Strand Road Junction to Amiens Street was completed, from when GS&WR locomotives worked in. The big 'Woolworth' moguls could use this route, but it would have meant two reversals in getting between the MGW and GS&WR lines via the Glasnevin and Drumcondra Junctions, and to obviate this a new connecting link was put in, but in the reverse direction to the original one, to enable MGW trains to pass direct on to the GS&WR line, and reach Amiens Street and Westland Row via North Strand Road Junction.

At the end of January 1937 the new link at Glasnevin was brought into use, and from that time the three expresses to the MGW line ran non-stop from Westland Row to Mullingar, though on the eastbound journey the corresponding trains made a call at Amiens Street. Close headway working was nothing new to the folks at Westland Row, and fortunately the MGW departures came at times when the station was not at its busiest with local traffic. A degree of reversible working was introduced, to enable the previous down through line platform, No 2, to be established also as the main departure platform for the west. The 7.10am Limited Mail, the 2.30pm and 7.00pm expresses for Galway, shortly after leaving took a facing crossover road on to the up line, before reaching and passing through Tara Street Station. The empty stock was previously stabled in the sidings just on the south-east side of Westland Row and drawn into the station by the train engine, almost always a Mogul. Complications sometimes arose if trains for the west had to be run in two or more section. Then the bay platform No 1 was sometimes called into use. This was normally used for the boat trains to Dun Laoghaire, but one might find the second part of a Galway express standing there with its train engine at the buffer stops. When the time for departure arrived the train would be propelled out on to the down Dun Laoghaire line, and further, over a crossover on to the up line. Then when all was clear the train was right away to Mullingar, passing through the up through line platform No 3 at Westland Row without stopping.

It was indicative of the effectiveness of the Moguls once thoroughly worked-in and subjected to their first heavy general overhauls either at Broadstone or Inchicore works, that despite the longer distance from Westland Row, and the complicated initial perambulation of the Dublin junction complex that the time to Mullingar was unchanged, 84 minutes non-stop for the run of $52\frac{1}{2}$ miles. The only two stopping trains, leaving Dublin at 9.15am and 5.45pm started from Amiens Street. The up Mail,

3.30pm from Galway, and 6.00pm from Mullingar, took 81 minutes to Amiens Street, and went through to Dun Laoghaire, arriving on the pier at 7.53pm. The fastest up train was the 8.45am Pullman car express from Galway, which ran from Mullingar to Amiens Street in 75 minutes.

It must have been gratifying to R. E. L. Maunsell, an Irishman himself, to see his Moguls being put to such good use in his native country, because in addition to their becoming the premier locomotives of the MGW section, they were also used on the Cork–Rosslare boat expresses, over a very difficult route. It was however, a little sad that his very first locomotive, the fine GSWR 4-4-0 No 341 *Sir William Goulding* should have been scrapped in 1928. But when Watson countermanded the order to build more of the design, even when matters had reached the stage of the frames being cut, the survival of No 341 as an isolated example was threatened. Although it was generally regarded, individually, as very successful, by the time the boiler was due for renewal it was no doubt considered uneconomic to perpetuate its life and though all locomotives engines of that vintage were long-lived there was, one can imagine, no case for spending much money on the renewal of No 341.

This chapter can be concluded by reference to the later history of the Connemara Class, which in their rebuildings became divided into the 536 and 540 Classes on the GSR, according to whether they had slide or piston valves. The dates quoted in the accompanying tables are those when the engines were superheated.

GSR (ex-MGW) 540 CLASS 4–4–0s (PISTON VALVES)

GSR number	MGW first number	MGW second number	Name	Date	Date withdrawn
540	7	7	*Connemara*	1917	*1953*
541	8	8	*St Patrick*	1917	1959
542	6	9	*Kylemore*	1917	1959
543	10	10	*Faugh-a-Ballagh*	1921	1959
544	11	11	*Erin-go-Bragh*	1926*	1955

*Date of rebuilding with large boiler

GSR (ex-MGW) 536 CLASS 4–4–0s (SLIDE VALVES)

GSR number	MGW first number	MGW second number	Name	Dates			Date with drawn
				A	B	C	
536	12	12	*Shamrock*	1925	1935	1938	1951
537	9	20	*Emerald Isle*	1922	1935	1940	1953
538	4	25	*Ballynahinch*	1924	—	1936	1950
539	5	26	*Croagh Patrick*	1924	1935	1939	1952

A – original boiler superheated
B – GSR standard X class boiler
C – 4ft 10in superheater boiler (as 540 Class)

The names were removed when the locomotives entered Great Southern Railways stock.

CHAPTER 12

Great Northern: Compounds and Caledonian Blue

Although certain partisans might disagree, I think it would be generally conceded that at the beginning of the 1930s the Midland compounds were the most successful 4-4-0s in British practice. While the Southern Schools were dimensionally the most powerful, they had not at that time risen to the heights of brilliance that put them subsequently in a class of their own. Therefore it was not altogether surprising that when more powerful locomotives were required to provide accelerated service on the Great Northern Railway of Ireland, and when physical circumstances made it desirable not to go beyond the 4-4-0 type, that consideration should have been given to an Irish adaptation of the basic Midland compound design. It is extremely interesting to set side by side the principal dimensions of Glover's new locomotives of 1932 and those of the standard 6ft 9in compounds of the LMS. Long experience of the latter, both in England and Scotland had already shown that they were at their best as much in the climbing of 1 in 100 gradients as they were in fast running over an undulating road with gradients of a give-and-take character. In this the Great Northern main line between Dublin and Belfast bears a striking resemblance to certain sections of the former Midland Railway in England.

In comparing dimensional details the most immediate difference to be noted was the use originally on the Irish locomotives of a much higher boiler pressure, and smaller cylinders, though the resulting tractive effort of the two designs works out at very much the same.

The chief difference structurally between the two designs was in respect of the firebox. The Midland version had a sloping grate, carried upwards to clear the rear coupled axle, while the Irish had a deep box with a flat grate set between the two coupled axles, giving a greater firebox volume and heating surface, but a smaller grate area. This involved setting the coupled axles 10ft

Plate 15(a) NCC: The first of Malcolm's superheated non-compound 4–4–0s of 1914, originally No 69, but here seen renumbered 71, named *Glenarm Castle*, and fitted with a Castle Class boiler. It still has the original short-wheelbase tender. (*L&GRP*)

(b) NCC: The first of the Moguls of 1933, No 90 *Duke of Abercorn*, maker of some remarkable runs on the Portrush service. (*L&GRP*)

Plate 16 The first of the GSR Queens, No 800 *Maeve*, at Cork Glanmire shed ready to work the English Mail to Dublin, when the author rode on the footplate. (*O. S. Nock*)

3-CYLINDER COMPOUND 4–4–0s

Railway	LMSR	GNR(I)
Cylinders: HP (1) dia, in	19	$17\frac{1}{4}$
LP (2) dia, in	21	19
stroke, in	26	26
Coupled wheel dia, ft in	6 – 9	6 – 7
Heating surface, sq ft:		
Tubes	1125.3	1089
Firebox	147.3	162
Superheater	290.7	277
Total	1563.3	1528
Grate area, sq ft	28.4	25.2
Boiler pressure, lb/sq in	200	250
Max axle load, tons	19.75	21.0
Total locomotive weight, tons	61.7	65
Locomotive and tender weight, tons	104.4	103.4
Tractive effort, lb	22,649	23,760

8in apart, as compared to 9ft 6in on the LMS locomotive, and placing the leading coupled axle 7ft 7in behind the rearmost bogie axle, as against 8ft 3in. The deep narrow firebox, with a flat grate, was of the type used on previous 4-4-0 locomotives of the Great Northern Railway of Ireland, and is one of the easiest to fire. Had the Midland design been adopted, some difficulty might have been expected at first while the firemen were acquiring the knack of dealing with a sloping grate of larger area. As it was, the crews took to the new locomotives very readily, and before 1932 was out many notable performances had been reported in the columns of *The Railway Magazine*. At first the five new locomotives were painted in the standard unlined black livery of the GNR(I), with the name in full on the tenders, and the coat of arms of the company. A feature welcomed by all enthusiasts was the resumption of naming, abandoned as a wartime economy. The five were named: 83 *Eagle*, 84 *Falcon*, 85 *Merlin*, 86 *Peregrine* and 87 *Kestrel*.

The capacity of the new locomotives was anticipated by some notable accelerations of the Dublin–Belfast service in the summer of 1932, when a total of no fewer than 20 runs were scheduled at start-to-stop average speeds of 54mph and over. As with one exception the distances between stops did not exceed 32 miles, it must be agreed that this involved some very smart work.

The timings concerned were:

GNR(I): RUNS AT 54mph AND OVER

From	To	No of trains	Miles	Time minutes	Average speed mph
Dublin	Dundalk	1	54.3	54	60.3
Drogheda	Dublin	2	31.7	32	59.4
Dublin	Drogheda	3	31.7	33	57.6
Drogheda	Dublin	1	31.7	33	57.6
Dundalk	Drogheda	2	22.6	24	56.5
Belfast	Portadown	2	24.9	27	55.3
Portadown	Belfast	1	24.9	27	55.3
Dublin	Drogheda	1	31.7	35	54.3
Drogheda	Dublin	2	31.7	35	54.3
Drogheda	Dundalk	3	22.6	25	54.2
Dundalk	Drogheda	2	22.6	25	54.2

Naturally it was the first of the above runs, made by the 3.15pm express out of Amiens Street, that provided the greatest attractions to the men with the stopwatches, and in the December 1932 issue of *The Railway Magazine* details of seven runs were published with loads rising from 245 up to 310 tons, reduced in each case by 35 tons intermediately by slipping a coach at Drogheda. On no occasion were any delays experienced en route, and only one one of the seven occasions was time not kept, then only to the extent of $1\frac{1}{4}$ minutes. On two runs the arrival in Dundalk was more than a minute early, and a particularly fine run was one in which Dundalk was reached in $53\frac{1}{2}$ minutes with a 310-ton load out of Dublin. On all trips very fast running was made after passing the summit of the climb out of the Boyne Valley – Kellystown signal box – with speeds up to 85mph. By a coincidence, the driver who lost a little time was one with whom I rode on the footplate four years later, and I found him one of the few who was not very enthusiastic about the compounds. He preferred the older Glover simple 4-4-0s, particularly those that had been fitted with boilers carrying a pressure of 200lb/sq in.

Nevertheless he drove No 85 *Merlin* in some style on the sharp 32-minute booking from Drogheda to Dublin, making a time of $30\frac{3}{4}$ minutes start-to-stop with a train of 275 tons. Out of seven runs on this schedule, on only one occasion did the start to stop

time get into the 31st minute. Even with a 330-ton train the time
was no more than 30 minutes 49 seconds. Over the mountain
section the work was generally less notable, because the
detaching of through carriages for Enniskillen, Bundoran, and
Londonderry at Dundalk on the northbound journey, and for
Warrenpoint at Goraghwood, reduced the loads to a minimum
for the heavily-graded section over Adavoyle summit. The
performance of the compounds generally, and the publicity they
received in the technical press, formed a magnificent finale to
Glover's career as locomotive engineer of the Great Northern. As
recorded in Chapter two of this book he retired in 1933 and the
management of the locomotive department was taken-over by
the chief civil engineer of the company, G. B. Howden. It was he
who conceived the idea of painting the five compounds in a
magnificent new livery of bright blue, almost identical in shade
to that of the Caledonian Railway in pre-grouping days, though
on the GNR(I) the red adopted for the underframes was nearer
scarlet than the purple-lake that used to adorn the Caledonian
passenger locomotives.

The new livery was adopted in 1936, and it was later that year
through Mr Howden's courtesy that I was privileged to make a
number of footplate trips on these engines. By that time,
however, with a view to reducing boiler maintenance charges the
pressure had been reduced to 200lb/sq in, a drastic step that had
necessitated the easing of some of the fastest schedules. The
tractive effort of the locomotives had been reduced to 19,000lb,
making them less powerful than the largest Glover simple 4-4-0s
that had had their pressure raised to 200lb/sq in. Nevertheless I
found the compounds very interesting and comfortable to ride,
and it was intriguing to hear the comments on them from drivers
at the three sheds concerned with express train operation on the
International main line. At the time of my journeys, although the
locomotives were working through between Dublin and Belfast,
re-manning took place at Dundalk on each trip. While the
Dublin and Belfast men did not go beyond Dundalk, those at the
latter station worked both north and south as the diagrams
required.

As everywhere in Great Britain and Ireland, one could note
variations in technique and attitude in the handling of
locomotives, and I was sorry not to encounter in my own

163

footplate journeys the most noted runners among the Dublin drivers of those days – undoubtedly Micky O'Farrell, and Paddy McBride. South of Dundalk, I rode with both Dublin and Dundalk drivers, whose work was sound without rising to the heights that the two drivers just mentioned often touched. As to variations, in June 1936 when I was spending a few days in the neighbourhood of Dundalk sightseeing as well as loco-spotting, I twice travelled to Goraghwood on the 9.00am train from Dublin, behind the same compound No 85 *Merlin* and with the same load of 235 tons, and the following brief table shows the astonishing variation in the running over this short section. To explain the speeds the gradients must be briefly mentioned, thus: roughly level for $1\frac{1}{4}$ miles out of Dundalk, 1 in 100 to Milepost 60, around 1 in 120 to Adavoyle, $\frac{1}{2}$ mile *down* at 1 in 140, to follow, and then 1 in 125 up to the summit at Milepost $65\frac{1}{2}$. Afterwards it is steeply down to Goraghwood. Then see what happened:

Run No		1		2	
Miles	Location	Time	Speed	Time	Speed
		min sec	mph	min sec	mph
0.0	*DUNDALK*	0 00	—	0 00	—
1.7	*Milepost 56*	3 33	45	3 27	45
3.7	*Milepost 58*	6 36	39	6 14	$40\frac{1}{2}$
5.7	*Milepost 60*	10 23	33	9 17	38
7.7	*Milepost 62*	13 46	$37\frac{1}{2}$	12 10	$42\frac{1}{2}$
8.2	*Adavoyle*	14 33	$52\frac{1}{2}$	12 52	$54\frac{1}{2}$
11.2	*Milepost $65\frac{1}{2}$*	18 25	45	16 25	$51\frac{1}{2}$
15.0	*Bessbrook*	21 48	79	19 58	69
17.6	*GORAGHWOOD*	24 26	—	23 09	—

One of my best runs with a compound was over this same section with the up Limited Mail when I was privileged to ride on the footplate. The start-to-stop booking of 38 minutes for the 33.4 miles from Portadown to Dundalk, with its average speed of 52.7mph, is a great deal harder than might be imagined, taking into account the $8\frac{1}{4}$-mile climb through the western ranges of the Mourne Mountains, on gradients mostly between 1 in 100 and 1 in 120. The first 13.7 miles to Milepost 74 are little removed from level, but intermediately severe speed restrictions are called for over the curves at Scarva and Poyntzpass stations. It needed very smart recoveries from these slacks to pass Goraghwood, 15.8 miles, in the scheduled 18 minutes from the Portadown

GNR(I): PORTADOWN–DUNDALK

Load: 230 tons tare; 245 tons full. Locomotive: 3-cylinder compound No 84 *Falcon*

Distance miles	Location	Schedule minutes	Actual min sec	Speed mph	Regulator opening	Cut-off HP %	Cut-off LP %	Steam pressure boiler	Steam pressure receiver
0.0	PORTADOWN	0	0 00		*First port	70	60	200	100
5.7	Tanderagee		7 14	67	Full			205	70
—			—	72	eased				
8.1	Scarva		9 25	slack	Full	60	50	205	70
—			—	65	eased	60	50		
10.8	Poyntzpass		12 18	slack	Full	60	50	205	70
13.7	*Milepost 74*		15 22	67½	Full	63	52		
15.8	GORAGHWOOD	18	17 25	58	Full	63	52	205	74
18.2	Milepost 69½		20 00	53	Full	65	54	205	74
20.2	Milepost 67½		22 29	45	Full	65	54		
22.2	Milepost 65½		25 20	40	eased	60	50	205	
26.2	Adavoyle	30	28 40	—	2/5	60	50	205	
29.7	*Mount Pleasant*		32 51	80½	2/5	60	50	205	
32.5	Milepost 55¼		34 56	82	closed				
33.4	DUNDALK	38	36 45	—	—				

*First port, and 70/60% cut-off used only for starting

start. The actual techniques of driving the compound engines was the same as that used on the Midland. I saw that drivers used a fully opened regulator only for the hardest uphill work, while the reversing gear operated the valves of both high- and low-pressure cylinders simultaneously. While boiler pressure had been reduced to a nominal 200lb/sq in in all the locomotives on which I rode, the valves did not blow-off until the needle had topped the 205lb/sq in mark.

I have set out the log of the run with the Limited Mail in some detail, because although notes on many runs have previously been published I am not aware of any that give particulars of the actual locomotive working. We had left Belfast with a substantial load of 305 tons, but the detaching of through carriages for Londonderry and Warrenpoint left us with 245 tons to take through the mountains. The locomotive did well in climbing the big bank, but speed was still falling as the summit was neared, and after the last adjustment of cut-off, the speeds at the end of successive miles were 53mph, 47½mph, 45mph, 42½mph, and finally 40mph. Even so, recalling what the Midland compounds could do, a load of 245 tons was not heavy by comparison. On an earlier occasion, when the locomotives still carried their full boiler pressure of 250lb/sq in and the drivers were working through between Dublin and Belfast, Micky O'Farrell on No 87 *Kestrel* hauling a gross load of 205 tons accelerated from a stop at Goraghwood to 48mph at the summit, passing Milepost 65½, 6.4 miles, in exactly 10 minutes. At one time it was customary to take the descent to Dundalk at no more than moderate speed, but towards the end of the 1930s (as I shall tell later) with the traditionally good permanent way of the Great Northern in superb condition, it became something of a race-track.

At the time I made my own footplate runs on the GNR(I) compounds I also spent some time walking the track and photographing the trains on this interesting stretch of line between Dundalk and Goraghwood. Favoured by good weather, a friend and I spent some pleasant days in that breezy upland country, and of the trains themselves I formed the impression that they were taking things quite easily on the steep rising gradients. One never seemed to see the spectacle of a locomotive being pounded for all it was worth up a bank, with the exhaust shooting skywards and rousing every echo for miles around, as one so often saw in England on Grayrigg bank. Going north several times, in my experience, drivers seemed to count upon the full 10 minutes for Customs examination at Goraghwood not being required. They would lose two or even three minutes on the climb from Dundalk, and still leave Goraghwood on time. And this is how it seemed with many northbound trains I saw from the lineside. On the other hand, southbound trains were coming down the bank like so many thunderbolts. I photographed Glover non-compound 4-4-0 No 190 tearing down the bank in most carefree style, and I was not surprised to hear from one of my Irish friends soon afterwards that he had clocked a maximum speed of no less than 90mph at this location.

Before leaving the compounds I must set on record two of their finest performances in the days of 250lb/sq in boiler pressure. The first was on the 3.15pm from Dublin when it ran non-stop to Dundalk in 54 minutes at a booked average speed of 60.3mph from start to stop. The minimum load was one of seven coaches, but with trains of up to nine it seemed to make little difference to the speeds run. One coach was slipped at Drogheda, reducing the load thence by 35 tons. The log presented herewith is a fine example of Micky O'Farrell's work, with No 84 *Falcon*.

GNR(I) 3.15pm DUBLIN–DUNDALK
Load: 9 coaches, 291 tons tare, 310 tons full
8 coaches, 259/275 tons from Drogheda

Distance		*Actual*		*Average speeds*
miles	*Location*	*min*	*sec*	*mph*
0.0	DUBLIN (AMIENS ST)	0	00	—
1.7	Clontarf	4	15	24.0
3.7	Raheny	7	04	42.6
4.8	*Howth Jcn*	8	12	58.1
6.7	Portmarnock	9	55	66.5
9.0	Malahide	11	56	68.5
11.4	Donabate	13	58	70.9
13.9	Rush & Lusk	16	03	71.8
16.0	*Milepost 16*	18	06	61.5
17.9	Skerries	19	52	64.6
21.7	Balbriggan	22	54	74.8
24.0	Gormanston	24	42	76.7
27.1	Laytown	27	10	75.3
30.3	*Milepost 30¼*	29	48	73.0

Distance miles	Location	Actual min	sec	Average speeds mph
31.7	DROGHEDA	31	30	49.4*
37.3	*Milepost 37¼*	39	04	44.4
41.7	Dunleer	42	59	67.5
43.6	Dromin Jcn	44	25	79.5
47.2	Castlebellingham	47	02	82.5
52.0	*Milepost 52*	50	45	61.3
54.3	DUNDALK	53	25	—

*Severe speed restriction through station and over Boyne viaduct

The principal maximum and minimum speeds were 73mph at Donabate, 58mph up the 1 in 180–173 rise to Milepost 16, 77½mph between Gormanstown and Laytown. Then from the slack through Drogheda speed was worked up to 50½mph on the 1 in 177 up to Milepost 37¼, while the racing descent past Dunleer to Castlebellingham produced a maximum of 86mph – a very splendid run with a start-to-stop average speed of 61mph.

In the reverse direction No 85 *Merlin* made an even faster run over the shorter distance of 31.7 miles from Drogheda into Dublin – 62.9mph with a train of 295 tons. Here is the log, and the average speeds:

Distance miles	Location	Actual min	sec	Average speeds mph
0.0	DROGHEDA	0	00	—
4.6	Laytown	6	16	44.1
7.7	Gormanston	8	54	70.5
10.0	Balbriggan	10	46	74.0
13.8	Skerries	13	59	70.9
15.7	*Milepost 16*	15	45	64.6
17.8	Rush & Lusk	17	31	71.5
20.3	Donabate	19	24	79.6
22.7	Malahide	21	18	76.0
26.9	*Howth Jcn*	24	53	70.5
28.0	Raheny	25	54	65.5
30.0	Clontarf	27	46	64.5
31.7	DUBLIN (AMIENS ST)	30	16	—

The principal maximum and minimum speeds were 75mph at Balbriggan, a minimum of 62mph at Milepost 16 and 82mph near Donabate.

It was in 1938 that renewal of the Glover superheated 4-4-0s of the 170 Class began. It was in no sense a 'rebuild', because practically everything was new. The new frames were the same thickness as the old ones, but 6in deeper, and were carried horizontally back from the highest part above the trailing axle, thus stiffening the rear end. This increased the weight of the locomotive by $1\frac{1}{4}$ tons, bringing the maximum axle-load up to 18 tons, and the adhesion to 35.3 tons. These locomotives, like all previous ones of the Great Northern, had been built down to a weight acceptable to the civil engineer, necessarily imposed by the design of the original viaduct over the River Boyne at Drogheda. It was the complete renewal of the main spans of this large structure that had enabled the maximum axle load of the compounds to be made as much as 21 tons. Welcome as was the strengthening of the frames, and the additional adhesion weight, the most important change was that made to the valve gear, increasing the maximum travel from $3\frac{3}{4}$in to 5in. Furthermore, the setting was such that even with a cut-off as much as 25 percent the full width of the port was open to exhaust. With the Stephenson's link motion, if the gear is linked up to really short cut-offs, such as are demanded by the theorists, it can produce a harsh and vibrating action, and drivers prefer to run at 22 or 25 percent, with a partly-closed regulator. With these renewed 170 Class, no lack of freedom or efficiency resulted from working at longer cut-offs than the theoretically ideal of 15 or 18 percent.

Enthusiasts were delighted to learn not only that the names originally borne by these locomotives were to be restored, but that they were to be painted in the splendid blue livery hitherto confined to the compounds. It will be recalled that it was only the first five of the class that bore names. The three that were built during the first world war were unnamed. These latter were also to be named like the others after mountains. The names allocated were:

170	*Errigal*	174	*Carrantuohill*
171	*Slieve Gullion*	190	*Luganquilla*
172	*Slieve Donard*	191	*Croagh Patrick*
173	*Galteemore*	192	*Slieve na Mon*

The first renewal to be completed was No 173, which was put into traffic in May 1938. It was followed by No 192 in June, No 171 in September, and No 172 in October. The remaining four followed in 1939.

I am afraid that those of us who followed Irish locomotive affairs from this side of the water did not at first appreciate the full significance of these renewals, gratifying though it was to learn of the blue painting and restoration of the names. But when friends returned from Ireland and brought news that Nos 173 and 192 were taking over some of the most important duties from the compounds it was time to take notice! Unfortunately the late summer and early autumn of 1938 were so filled with alarms from the continent of Europe, culminating in the Munich Crisis, that expeditions far from home and business headquarters were out of the question. But in November, when things had quietened down again and a point requiring a visit to Belfast had arisen in my ordinary work, I conceived the idea of going via Holyhead and Dun Laoghaire, instead of via Heysham. I had learned that No 173 was regularly on the 6.40am Mail from Dublin, and the 5.40pm up and by using the former train I could be in Belfast by 9.10am. The Great Northern readily gave me a footplate pass; but what I did not bargain for was that a minor crisis blew up that required my immediate attention in Manchester the day before I was due in Belfast. So instead of proceeding to Holyhead in the normal manner, I had to catch the 10.20pm from Manchester, without any chance of a sleeper and then face that unspeakable change from train to boat at Holyhead at 2.00am on a December morning!

I was then forty years younger, taking such hazards in my stride, and then thoroughly enjoyed my footplate ride on *Galteemore*, to be described later. My signalling business with the NCC involved a trip to Coleraine, but from the outset it seemed that my Belfast friends were out to make a gala occasion of it. Signalling matters were quickly and satisfactorily disposed of, but my heart sank when it was announced that we were going on to Portrush for lunch. It was essential for me to catch the 2.50pm train back to Belfast, in order to pick up my return working on the up Limited Mail of the GNR(I) and in the festive mood that was rapidly developing there seemed a very good chance of missing that vital 2.50pm, particularly as our luncheon venue was a good ten minutes' walk from the station. However, by urging my kindly hosts to aid their digestions by running most of the way, we scrambled into the train just as it was moving. Later that night I was mighty glad that a bed awaited me in the station hotel at Holyhead!

To revert to *Galteemore* and its running on the Limited Mail Howden's drawing office at Dundalk sent me a diagram of the renewed locomotive, with details of the valve setting, which made it clear why drivers preferred to keep the cut-off around the 25 percent mark, and 'drive on the regulator'. I found it a delightful locomotive – fast, free and very economical. There was a heavy permanent way slack in store for us between Malahide and Donabate, but that did prevent us keeping, save for a few seconds, the sharp initial booking of 33 minutes, for the 31.7 miles to Drogheda. Naturally, in mid-winter, the load was down to its minimum of seven vehicles, including breakfast car and through carriage and postal van from Dun Laoghaire, but I was impressed with the way the locomotive ran at 75mph to 78mph on virtually level track north of Skerries, until the 1 in 300 rising approach to Drogheda was struck. The driver set the reverser to give 32 percent cut-off, and never varied the position, making all variations on the regulator. He made a very smart run to Dundalk, covering the 22.6 miles in $24\frac{1}{4}$ minutes start-to-stop, with a maximum speed of 82mph at Castlebellingham.

The Dundalk driver who took over did not exert the locomotive on the steep climb to Adavoyle, and lost three minutes to Goraghwood, but Customs formalities were quickly concluded, and we left on time. The addition of the Londonderry through coach at Portadown brought the load up to 275 tons, and on the generally adverse length following we dropped a minute on the sharp allowance of seven minutes to the Lurgan stop, 4.9 miles. We ran smartly on the final length into Belfast, mostly downhill, and made the 20-mile run in 23 minutes start-to-stop, arriving two minutes early. Later that day I was glad that my NCC friends succumbed to post-prandial sleep once we landed in that vital 2.50pm from Portrush, because I too was by then in need of a little relaxation. The run up to Belfast was one of the few on which my stopwatch did not go into action, and by the time we arrived at York Road and I had taxied across the city to Great Victoria Street, I was ready to enjoy another spell on the footplate of *Galteemore*.

The day had been crisp and fine, and as usual at that time of year there was a tendency for mist to thicken after nightfall. Otherwise we had a splendid run throughout to Dublin. The

Belfast driver who worked the train as far as Dundalk ran with
the reverser in 22 percent cut-off for most of the way, using 27
per cent only on the final stages of the climb to the summit near
Adavoyle. No through carriages were taken in the winter
months, so we had no more than seven coaches from the start.
The log of the run is set out in the accompanying table. The
misty conditions developing in the still frosty air only affected
our approaches to Dundalk and Drogheda. In the latter case we
ran very cautiously, where at other times speeds rose to around
80mph. The locomotive was worked fairly easily up the bank
from Goraghwood, with cut-off not advanced beyond 27
percent, but we ran very freely down towards Dundalk, touching
$86\frac{1}{2}$mph before we approached the fog area. On another occasion
Galteemore was driven a little harder up the bank, not falling
below 38mph at Milepost $65\frac{1}{2}$, and this was followed by a terrific
descent to Dundalk, with a top speed of 90mph. Continuing to
Dublin on my own run, with an old friend Paddy Muckian as
driver, we got away very smartly. Climbing the six-mile bank at
1 in 197 to Kellystown at a minimum speed of $50\frac{1}{2}$mph, we had
ample time in hand for a punctual arrival in Drogheda had it not
been for the fog rolling up from the Boyne valley. But with a fine
concluding sprint we clocked into Dublin dead on time. I made
my way rearwards to the Dun Laoghaire through carriage, and
the run down to the pier gave me time to make myself
presentable again before boarding the mail boat for Holyhead.

Although it is carrying the story a few years beyond the span
covered generally in this book, I should mention that after the
second world war the Great Northern took delivery of five new
express passenger three-cylinder 4-4-0s from Beyer Peacock &
Co. They were the only locomotives of that category to be
introduced on Irish railways after the Great Southern Queens of
1939, and the last steam types. It was interesting that the Great
Northern should have reverted, in concluding the steam saga, to
simple expansion; although looking so very like the Glover
compounds these locomotives were three-cylinder simples with
$15\frac{1}{4}$in by 26in cylinders, and carrying a boiler pressure of
220lb/sq in. Like everywhere else in the British Isles schedules
had been very much decelerated during the war, and afterwards
unfortunately no opportunity came my way of seeing the new
locomotives at work.

GNR(I) BELFAST–DUBLIN
The Up Limited Mail in December 1938
Load: to Dundalk: 7 coaches, 211 tons tare, 225 tons full
Load: to Dublin: 8 coaches, 242 tons tare, 260 tons full
Locomotive: 4–4–0 No 173 *Galteemore*

Distance miles	*Location*	*Schedule minutes*	*Actual min*	*sec*	*Speeds mph*
0.0	BELFAST (Great Victoria St)	0	0	00	–
2.3	Balmoral		5	42	$41\frac{1}{2}$
7.6	LISBURN	12	12	30	53
14.5	Moira		19	18	$67\frac{1}{2}/58\frac{1}{2}$
20.0	LURGAN		24	24	$71\frac{1}{2}$
24.0	*Seagoe Box*		27	50	76
24.9	PORTADOWN	30	29	10	
5.7	Tanderagee		7	12	$71\frac{1}{2}$
10.8	Poyntzpass		12	13	slack
15.8	GORAGHWOOD	18	18	20	$68\frac{1}{2}/54\frac{1}{2}$
18.4	Bessbrook		21	25	45
22.2	*Milepost $65\frac{1}{2}$*		27	29	34
25.2	Adavoyle	30	30	47	$70\frac{1}{2}$
32.5	*Milepost $55\frac{1}{4}$*		36	28	$86\frac{1}{2}$
33.4	DUNDALK	38	38	22	–
7.1	Castlebellingham		8	23	$71\frac{1}{2}$
12.6	Dunleer		13	38	60
17.0	*Kellystown Box*		18	33	$50\frac{1}{2}$
–			FOG		
22.6	DROGHEDA	25	25	58	
4.6	Laytown		6	36	69
10.0	Balbriggan		11	32	66
13.8	Skerries		15	03	$64\frac{1}{2}$
15.7	*Milepost 16*		16	53	$58\frac{1}{2}$
20.3	Donabate		20	58	78
22.7	Malahide		23	00	66/71
26.9	*Howth Jcn*		26	41	67
30.0	Clontarf		29	37	60
31.7	DUBLIN (AMIENS ST)	34	32	23	

CHAPTER 13

NCC: The Speir Effect

It is often averred that the mere suggestion that a line is to be electrified gives an immediate boost to traffic. The 'sparks effect' once promise has become actuality, has been proved an hundredfold. The similarity to the situation on the Northern Counties Committee line of the LMS has prompted me to title this chapter *The Speir Effect* because the magic hand of Major Malcolm Speir, its Manager and Secretary, had a positively electrifying effect upon every department and every unit from end to end of the line. Many eminent railwaymen will be remembered for their drive. Speir did not drive, he led, admittedly sometimes at an almost breakneck speed. Although this is a book primarily about locomotives Speir as the absolutely complete railwayman, appreciated that the steam locomotive was his principal tool of operation; in studying NCC activities in the later 1930s one came to realise how the split-second timings of certain of the operations were so completely dependent on the performance of the locomotives, and the efficient handling of them by the crews.

It was not without significance that although he was born a Highland Scot, his early training from the age of 18 was on the Midland Railway at the time when that incomparable operator Cecil W. Paget was instituting his principles of train control. After his early training Speir had a brief spell in the USA and returned to join the Caledonian Railway, on which in a very short time he had made sufficient a mark to be appointed Outdoor Assistant Superintendent of the line at the age of 25. When war came in August 1914, although he was in what in the 1939–45 war would have been called a 'reserved occupation' he volunteered at once, was commissioned in the Royal Engineers, and was in France as early as September 1914. He served throughout the war, and in the course of a distinguished career in which he was twice mentioned in despatches and awarded the Military Cross, he was promoted eventually to

174

Major, and in 1919 returned to his former post on the Caledonian Railway. On the formation of the LMS in 1923 he was appointed Assistant General Superintendent Northern Division, and continued to be known as Major Speir, largely to distinguish him from his elder brother, Colonel Speir, who held an important post in the headquarters organisation of the LMS at Euston.

He was appointed Manager and Secretary of the NCC in 1931, and he had not been there very long before he had to withstand all the storm and stress of the prolonged and bitter railway strike that affected all the railways of Northern Ireland in 1933. It was when W. A. Willox, Editor of *The Railway Magazine*, decided to make the May issue of every year a special Irish number, and commissioned me to do a series of articles on NCC affairs that I got to know Speir so well. Willox as an ROD officer had known him during the war, and sent a letter of introduction to him in advance, so that on my first arrival at the York Road offices in Belfast not only was I greeted most cordially by Speir himself, but by a 'levee' of his chief officers, summoned to be advised of my commission, and briefed as to the assistance each and all should give me. In the course of this he contrived to give me a lightning sketch of the multifarious activities of the whole railway, with pointers as to items he thought worthy of special notice. Before that commission was finished I must have made ten or a dozen visits to Northern Ireland, but every time he always contrived to greet me personally, even though there was often time for no more than a cordial shake of the hand. Up and down the line 'The Major', as he was everywhere known, was far more than the boss. He was the 'father figure', affectionately regarded, as well as revered for his masterly grip on every detail of the running of the line. I came to realise that he was not only a great railwayman, but was also a great Christian gentleman.

When I first went to the NCC in 1935 his organisation, built up from the difficult days of 1933, was already worked up to concert pitch. The completion of the Greenisland loop line had enabled the time of the best Belfast–Portrush expresses to be cut to 80 minutes for the run of 65.2 miles, inclusive of one stop. It was not only the new loop line that helped. From his long experience of operating in Scotland, Major Speir was aware of the time that could be lost in slowing down for single-line passing

175

places, even though many of these were well aligned, as on the former Highland Railway. On the NCC, although the loops were equipped with the Manson mechanical tablet-exchanging apparatus, the alignment of the junctions was not such as to permit full-speed running. Speir arranged for bi-directional running on both tracks at all the loops between Ballymena and Portrush, and for the through line, used for all non-stopping trains in both directions to be re-aligned and made straight, with no speed restriction, while the other line serving the station platform had relatively sharp turnouts at each end. With this facility the exchanging of tablets often took place at nearly 70mph. But I am anticipating – I have not yet referred to the locomotives mainly responsible for the maintenance of Major Speir's enterprising timetables.

While the normal loads of the fastest trains were no more than light and could be timed readily enough by the 4-4-0 superheated locomotives of the Castle class, the Portrush service was designed to attract holiday traffic, which automatically involves peak loading, and something larger than 4-4-0 locomotives was desirable. To what extent there were consultations with the LMS I do not know, but the new 2-6-0s introduced in 1933 even at an outside glance bore many resemblances to current practice at Derby. The design was based on the highly successful 2-6-4 passenger tank engines of the 2300 Class, which although having coupled wheels of only 5ft 9in diameter frequently attained speeds of more than 80mph on the outer suburban trains to and from Euston. But the Irish 2-6-0 version of the design had 6ft 0in driving wheels in keeping with the standard practice for 4-4-0 express locomotives on the NCC. Except for this, the basic dimensions were the same: cylinders 19in by 26in, and boiler pressure 200lb/sq in, which gave a nominal tractive effort of 22,160lb. The total evaporative heating surface was a little less than that of the LMS 2-6-4 tanks, namely 1081sq ft against 1220, but the superheater and grate area were the same. Although thus following a Derby design of the Fowler era, evidence of the incoming Stanier influence was to be seen in the provision of top-feed apparatus.

The broad outlines of the new locomotives were worked out at Belfast while H. P. Stewart was Locomotive Engineer. His successor, M. Patrick, took office at about the same time as the first of the new locomotives was put into traffic in July 1933. The outstanding success of the LMS 2-6-4 tanks was in large part due to the cylinder and piston valve design, and the setting of the Walschaerts gear, which provided for a maximum travel of $6\frac{3}{8}$ in in full gear. This was followed exactly on the NCC 2-6-0s, with equally beneficial results. The first, No 90, was named *Duke of Abercorn* shortly after its arrival in Belfast; but Nos 91, 92 and 93, delivered in 1933, were at first unnamed. No 96, delivered in 1935, was appropriately named *Silver Jubilee*, after the great Royal event of the year, while No 97 became *Earl of Ulster*. The naming of the rest of the class took place in 1936, and the additional locomotives up to No 100 were named as they were introduced, as follows:

90	*Duke of Abercorn*	96	*Silver Jubilee*
91	*The Bush*	97	*Earl of Ulster*
92	*The Bann*	98	*King Edward VIII*
93	*The Foyle*	99	*King George VI*
94	*The Maine*	100	*Queen Elizabeth*
95	*The Braid*		

Four more of the class were added in the early years of the war.

I had many opportunities of observing the work of these locomotives at first hand from the footplate. It was a time when a great many of the more technically-minded of railway enthusiasts were flogging the precept that the only correct way to drive a locomotive was to use an absolutely full opening of the regulator, and make all adjustments of power requirement by varying the point of cut-off in the cylinders. My own footplate experiences, not only in Ireland but on some of the latest and most successful British locomotives, threw the theorists into some confusion, none more so than the magnificent results I recorded with the Schools class 4-4-0s of the Southern Railway, most of which I found were driven in flat contradiction of this theory! How could this be so, in view of the outstandingly good performances of these locomotives? A point of the utmost importance, to which the theorists of those days seemed to pay little or no heed, was that the exhaust end of the cycle of events in a steam locomotive cylinder is just as vital theoretically as the inlet.

In the previous chapter, dealing with the renewed superheater 4-4-0s of the Great Northern 170 Class, I mentioned that the modified valve setting applied to these gave a full-port exhaust opening at 25 percent cut-off, and that drivers found they eliminated vibration off the motion when working in this position, with a partly-closed regulator. The locomotives were very fast and free-running, and very economical when worked in this way; my first experience on the footplate of one of the NCC 2-6-0s was similar. The train was the Portrush Flyer on its summer timing, including one stop at Portstewart within the 80-minute overall allowance, and conveying a substantial load of 290 tons. The locomotive was No 93, at that time unnamed. The driver did not use more than a three-fifths opening of the main regulator valve, and ran with a cut-off of 18 to 20 percent on the faster stretches of line, at 60mph to 65mph. Even in climbing the 1 in 76 gradient on the Greenisland loop line he did not use a wider regulator opening, and increased cut-off to 40 percent. On this bank, a slightly shorter version of Shap on the West Coast main line, but commenced at much lower speed, the minimum speed was 24½mph. Delays prevented time being kept to Portrush, but the net time was comfortably inside schedule. I kept a very careful check on the coal consumption on this run, and my estimate was that it did not exceed 26lb/mile – a very economical figure.

One of my NCC friends in Belfast sent me details of a run he made on No 96 *Silver Jubilee* on The Golfer's Express, which made an intermediate stop at Ballymoney. This had the minimum load of these 80-minute Portrush expresses, totalling no more than 185 tons behind the tender. This driver evidently believed in working with a very narrow regulator opening. For Greenisland bank he used one half of the main valve, with no less than 47 percent cut-off, and once over the top of the bank with a downhill run almost to Ballymena he changed over to the first port of the regulator, giving a very narrow opening, and kept the cut-off at 40 percent. The locomotive ran freely enough, using practically no steam, and passed Ballymena, 31.0 miles, in 36¼ minutes, nearly two minutes early. Then, in most extraordinary contrast, there was my own first run on the North Atlantic Express, which had a sharp timing of 35 minutes to its first stop at Ballymena. This again conveyed a load of 185 tons, and was hauled by the pioneer locomotive No 90 *Duke of Abercorn*. The driver was John Young, and the run he gave me still remains one of the most remarkable in all my footplate experience, even if it was made 47 years ago.

Along the shore of Belfast Lough we got away in great style, passing Whitehouse, 3.3 miles in a shade over five minutes, at 54mph; then came the heavy ascent over the loop line. With full regulator and 40 percent cut-off, the bank, was mounted at a sustained $36\frac{1}{2}$mph and we passed the summit at Ballyclare Junction, 8.2 miles from Belfast, in $12\frac{1}{4}$ minutes. For the long descent to Antrim cut-off was first of all shortened to 10 percent, then as soon as we had attained 60mph Young changed over to the first port of the regulator. As we approached Templepatrick, as if this were not easy enough steaming, the locomotive was still further notched up to 7 percent cut-off. The speed steadily rose, until approaching the foot of the incline near Muckamore we were doing $71\frac{1}{2}$mph. Even with a load of only 190 tons this was remarkable going with only 7 percent cut-off; it should be remembered too that only the first port of the regulator was being used. At Antrim the driver changed over to full regulator, and at Cookstown Junction in readiness for the gradually-rising grades to Ballymena, cut-off was advanced to 10 percent. Even this was easy working for uphill running, yet the two miles at 1 in 214 beyond Kellswater were mounted at a minimum speed of $52\frac{1}{2}$mph and we reached Ballymena, our only stop, in exactly the 35 minutes allowed.

Although such very early cut-offs were the general order of the day, Driver Young did not spare the locomotive when occasion demanded, and we fairly roared up the 1 in 100 rise out of Ballymena on full regulator and no less than 50 percent cut-off. As might be imagined, this produced a rapid acceleration, speed rising to 43mph in one mile from the start. A stretch of undulating line follows, the tendency of which is definitely 'against the collar', but nevertheless cut-off was brought back to 10 percent. We passed Cullybackey, 2.9 miles from the restart, in exactly five minutes, and then approaching Glarryford, advantage was taken of a short length of falling grade to notch up to the rather astonishing figure of five percent. Never in the whole of my experience have I noted such a short cut-off. The regulator remained absolutely full open and speed mounted to

61mph. Down the steep bank to Ballymoney the first regulator only was used, but with this exception and a brief spell at 10 per cent after Coleraine, five percent with a full open regulator was used throughout from Glarryford to Portrush, and sufficed to maintain an average speed of 52mph. Thus the run from Belfast was completed in 78 minutes.

My first reaction to the cut-offs indicated on the reverser-scale on this locomotive was just disbelief. I knew that the LMS 2-6-4 tanks working the Watford–Euston residential trains were often pulled up to as little as 10 percent cut-off but *five per cent* was just 'not on', as the modern colloquialism has it. On arrival at Portrush I spent a little time on the footplate, and Driver Young assured me that No 90 would run just as well in 5 percent backward gear. This seemed to dispel any idea that the marking on the reverser scale was wrong. Furthermore in subsequent correspondence with Major Speir I learned that the No 90 had run 100,000 miles since first going into traffic two years earlier, and that it had not had any overhaul in the intervening years. I wrote a short article about this run, and sent it to Major Speir for his approval before passing it on to *The Railway Gazette*. He sent it back without comment, except to include a drawing of the cylinders, piston valves and valve gear of these locomotives. *The Railway Gazette* published it in October 1935, and then the fun started! I did not hear of the furore that was created until I next went to Belfast. Then, apparently, railwaymen of every estate descended in a cloud upon the locomotive department of the NCC. The comment was just about evenly balanced between those who said it was a sheer impossibility, and those who praised the efficiency of the locomotive.

The article in *The Railway Gazette* was unsigned, so I was not at first drawn into it. Patrick, the locomotive superintendent, was on the side of the doubters. My friend Willie Marshall, who was personal assistant to the Major, was equally doubtful because it cut so completely across his own personal footplate experience of those locomotives. Eventually an appeal was made to the Major himself. He, with characteristic straight-forwardness, said simply, 'Ask the driver. Get him to come here, and I'll talk to him'. Driver Young ushered into the presence was apparently completely unabashed and said straight away that he had worked in five percent, but added at once that

No 90 was the only one of the class that he would care to work thus. The calibration of the scale was checked and found to be quite accurate. But the significant point that emerged was that the recorded coal consumption of this locomotive, which others beside Driver Young were in the habit of working at very short cut-offs, was not appreciably different from other engines of the class. They were all extremely economical. On my run with No 90 I estimated that the coal consumption was no more than 21lb/mile.

NCC BELFAST–PORTRUSH

Locomotive: No		96		90		79	
	Name	*Silver Jubilee*		*Duke of Abercorn*		*Kenbaan Castle*	
Type		2–6–0		2–6–0		4–4–0	
Load tons, empty/full		175/185		176/185		179/190	
Distance		*min*	*sec*	*min*	*sec*	*min*	*sec*
miles	*Location*						
0.0	BELFAST	0	00	0	00	0	00
3.3	Whitehouse	6	00	5	08	5	55
4.6	*Bleach Green Jcn*	7	40	6	48	7	37
7.0	Mossley	11	15	10	12	11	40
8.2	Ballyclare Jcn	13	05	12	10	13	50
10.9	Doagh	16	05	15	28	16	55
13.9	Templepatrick	18	50	18	23	19	47
17.3	Muckamore	21	45	21	23	22	26
19.3	ANTRIM	23	35	23	08	24	03
22.4	Cookstown Jcn	26	50	26	08	26	47
26.7	Kellswater	31	30	30	36	30	40
31.0	BALLYMENA	36	10	35	33	35	17
33.9	Cullybackey	40	00	5	00	6	06
38.7	Glarryford	44	55	9	55	11	02
40.9	Killagan	47	15	12	15	13	10
—		sigs		–		–	
43.6	Dunloy	51	40	15	17	15	50
50.9	BALLYMONEY	61	00	22	55	22	16
54.6	Macfin	5	10	27	03	25	50
59.2	COLERAINE	9	45	32	12	30	08
62.5	Portstewart	13	35	36	27	33	35
65.2	PORTRUSH	17	25	40	20	37	25

So far as times and speeds were concerned the running of No 90 was handsomely beaten by another run I had on the same train, when it was hauled by one of the Castle series of superheater 4-4-0s, and I have tabulated this alongside the two 2-6-0 runs with the same load, when the driving techniques used on Nos 90 and 96 were so very different. The working on the latter, referred to earlier, was the particular driver's method. I had a run on the footplate of the same locomotive from Portrush to Belfast, with a much heavier train of 315 tons, and saw it linked up to cut-offs of 12 and 15 percent for the fast-running sections of the line. The three runs tabulated, while showing consistent and commendable timekeeping are equally interesting, particularly in respect of the first two, as to the divergences in driving practice that can yield such similar results. Nos 96 and 90 it will be seen made almost identical times over the 23.4 miles between Whitehouse and Kellswater, and exactly so between Cullybackey and Killagan. Yet on this latter stretch No 96 was being worked in 40 percent cut-off with the first port of the regulator, and No 90 at first had 10 percent and then 5 percent cut-off, with absolutely full regulator! On average the section is rising, with some short stretches as steep as 1 in 117, but the average speeds were precisely the same in both cases, namely 57.9mph.

It was clear to me that these 2-6-0s had a great amount of power in reserve, if only by comparison of the time made between Cullybackey and Killagan by the 4-4-0 No 79 *Kenbaan Castle* in the third column of the table – by a few seconds the fastest of all three. In commenting on these runs in *The Railway Magazine* back in 1937, Cecil J. Allen said that the 4-4-0 would be at a disadvantage, 'through having larger driving wheels'; this, of course, was a wrong assumption because all the passenger locomotives of the NCC had the same size, namely 6ft 0in coupled wheels. *Kenbaan Castle* somewhat naturally dropped behind a little on the 1 in 76 ascent of the Greenisland loop line, but in spite of wind and rain the speed did not fall below 30mph sustained up the last mile of the steepest grade. The initial allowance of 12 minutes to Ballyclare Junction is nevertheless very sharp and we dropped nearly two minutes. This was the Saturday working, when the North Atlantic Express left at midday. I was not on the footplate on this occasion, but instead enjoying lunch in the dining car. I must admit however that when the driver began to make full use of the falling gradients to recover the initial loss of time the riding became distinctly lively; the 2-6-0s had drifted downhill in the most nonchalant style. *Kenbaan Castle* worked up to a well sustained 75mph, to clock into Ballymena on time.

The train was kept waiting three minutes over time at Ballymena, and although the restart was not so vigorous as that of the *Duke of Abercorn* the 4-4-0 was going strongly enough from Cullybackey, and on passing Ballymoney it had overtaken and drawn ahead of the former locomotive's times. The speed had risen to 76½mph descending the bank from Dunloy, and after easing through Ballymoney, the driver continued to make a very fast finish, covering the last 14.3 miles into Portrush in no more than 15 minutes 9 seconds. This includes a bank 2½ miles long immediately after Coleraine, inclined at 1 in 121–179, while after the Ballymoney slack speed rose again to 69mph on virtually level track after Macfin. Thus despite the delay at Ballymena the train arrived in Portrush 1¾ minutes early. The start-to-stop average speed of 54.5mph made by running the 34.2 miles from Ballymena in 37 minutes 25 seconds was over a section single-tracked throughout, with mechanical tablet-exchanging not only at all intermediate stations but at crossing loops as well. Tablet-exchanging can be a slightly hazardous business even with an apparatus so well proved as the Manson; on one occasion when I was on the footplate of an NCC 2-6-0 the cab apparatus jammed, and we had to stop and send the fireman running back to collect the tablet.

In the reverse direction I had two interesting runs on The Portrush Flyer, in different conditions of loading. The first was a winter occasion when the train calls at Coleraine, and I joined it there, after attending to some signalling business. The locomotive to my great interest was one of the 18-inch rebuilds of a light compound, though having the same type of boiler as the Castle Class. The second run when I was on the footplate was a summer Saturday evening occasion, when the train was crowded with returning holidaymakers. On the first of the two runs No 4 *Glenariff* ran well up to the standard required on the 80-minute Portrush expresses, although having a considerably lower tractive effort than the 2-6-0s – 18in by 24in cylinders against 19in by 26in, and 170lb/sq in pressure against 200lb/sq in. The line from Coleraine to Ballymoney is slightly adverse, but a maximum of 62½mph was attained after Macfin. On the second run, *Silver Jubilee* with the substantial load of 315 tons made rather heavy weather of the steeply adverse initial climb to Portstewart, but got away well from this stop and just kept the sharp timing of 16 minutes for the 11.6 miles to Ballymoney. I noticed that this driver kept the regulator full open, and made frequent adjustments of cut-off to suit the equally frequent changes in gradient, mostly between 15 and 22 per cent.

Direct comparison between the two runs begins at Ballymoney, from which both locomotives were starting dead up the severe ascent to Milepost 48. The gradients vary mostly between 1 in 97 and 1 in 139, and continue for just over five miles. After topping this rise the inclination is slightly falling, though the line is so much beset by curves, not to mention the incidence of tablet-exchanging, that any really fast running is out of the question. The Glen Class locomotives have the same maximum load limit on passenger trains as the Castles, despite their smaller cylinders. For these 4-4-0s it was 255 tons, as against the 330 tons laid down for the 2-6-0s, and with the respective tractive efforts at 16064lb and 22160lb the loads per ton of tractive effort were almost identical, at 35.7 tons and 35.0 tons. From these considerations *Glenariff* did the better work up the Ballyboyland bank, attaining 44mph on the upper part, and then practically keeping time to Ballymena, despite a relaying check near Dunloy. Maximum speed afterwards was 67mph. On the summer occasion *Silver Jubilee* was worked in 40 percent cut-off at first, and then 35 percent to the top of the bank, where speed had reached 40mph; the downhill stretch following was taken so gently, with an average of only 56mph from Dunloy to Cullybackey, that nearly a minute was dropped on schedule.

On the last stage into Belfast, where the Portrush Flyer had a schedule three minutes easier than the North Atlantic Express, principal interest centred in the climbing of the long bank from Antrim up to Kingsbog Junction, 10½ miles, the average inclination is about 1 in 250, but the last 4½ miles are almost continuously at 1 in 180. *Glenariff* got a bad start from a severe permanent way check but recovered well to 63mph before

Antrim, then averaging 50½mph as far as Doagh, where a second permanent way check was experienced. *Silver Jubilee* got away from Ballymena in excellent style, passing Antrim at 69mph. The driver, McNally of Belfast shed, was an artist of an engineman. Keeping the regulator full open he made constant adjustments of cut-off to suit the varying gradients on the climb, finally advancing to 30 percent to take the 315-ton train over Kingsbog summit at 47½mph. No more than moderate speeds were run on the steep descent over the Greenisland loop line, and despite the two checks the train was less than a minute late on the first run and a little before time on the second.

At the time when I was doing most of my travelling on the NCC line there were only eight of the 2-6-0s in service, and the working of the sharply-timed Larne boat expresses was entirely in the hands of 4-4-0 locomotives. To cover the 24.3 miles down to Larne Harbour in the level half-hour was no sinecure, because one had almost from the start the four-mile climb to Greenisland, three-quarters of which was at 1 in 97–156. Then came the single-line section from Whitehead, with a moderate slack at Magheramorne loop and a very severe one at Larne town. It was said that most of the boat train drivers went round Magheramorne curve 'on one wheel', but at Larne it was always thrilling to hear the way locomotives were opened-up afterwards, 'flat out', for the last mile over the causeway to the Harbour station. Not the least bit of excitement on this run was to witness the transhipment from train to boat. The station had a single island platform, and by use of a belt conveyor the transfer of luggage and mails had been reduced to split-second timing, and the schedule time between arrival of the train and the departure of the boat was *eight minutes* – the 'Speir effect' indeed!

Details of two excellent runs on the boat trains are tabulated, the first being with one of the Mountain Class rebuilt 4-4-0s, No 62 *Slemish*, having 18-in cylinders but the smaller standard boiler, and 175lb/sq in pressure. The locomotive was worked very hard at first, not falling below 47½mph on the Greenisland bank, and the curving coastal section was taken moderately until Magheramorne was passed; but then the locomotive was steamed hard again to Larne Town and time just kept. This was on the evening train, which makes connection across the water to

Glasgow, Newcastle and London; but the morning train was perhaps the more impressive from the operational point of view, because it used the coaching stock from the North Atlantic Express. When I made the trip the latter train was booked in at 9.29am, and the boat train away at 9.37am – more 'Speir' effects. I rode down to Larne on No 81 *Carrickfergus Castle*, and it was an exciting experience. The locomotive was worked in 32

NCC PORTRUSH–BELFAST

Locomotive: No		4	96
	Name	*Glenariff*	*Silver Jubilee*
Type		4–4–0	2–6–0
Load tons, empty/full		176/185	287/315
Distance miles	Location	min sec	min sec
0.0	PORTRUSH	—	0 00
2.7	Portstewart	—	7 55
3.3/0.0	COLERAINE	0 00	6 18
4.6	Macfin	7 32	11 28
7.3	BALLYMONEY	11 35	15 50
3.4	*Milepost 50*	7 08	7 41
5.4	*Milepost 48*	10 02	10 50
7.3	Dunloy	12 12	13 26
—		pws	—
10.0	Killagan	15 32	16 40
12.2	Glarryford	18 04	18 58
17.0	Cullybackey	22 49	23 47
19.9	BALLYMENA	26 13	26 55
—		pws	—
4.3	Kellswater	6 02	6 07
8.6	Cookstown Jcn	12 13	10 33
11.7	ANTRIM	15 25	13 22
15.1	Dunadry	19 05	16 39
17.1	Templepatrick	21 26	18 54
20.1	Doagh	25 22	22 33
—		pws	—
21.8	*Kingsbog Jcn*	27 53	24 41
27.7	Whitehouse	35 00	30 57
31.0	BELFAST	38 46*	36 05

*Net time 35 minutes

NCC BELFAST–LARNE HARBOUR

Locomotive: No		62		81	
	Name	*Slemish*		*Carrickfergus Castle*	
Load, tons empty/full		163/175		174/185	

Distance miles	*Location*	*min*	*sec*	*min*	*sec*
0.0	BELFAST	0	00	0	00
3.3	Whitehouse	6	18	5	31
4.6	Bleach Green Jcn	7	54	7	09
6.7	Greenisland	10	28	9	35
9.7	CARRICKFERGUS	13	52	12	33
11.6	Kilroot	15	52	14	21
14.7	Whitehead	19	11	17	19
—		—		pws	
16.6	Ballycarry	21	07	20	19
19.8	Magheramorne	24	11	23	38
21.6	Glynn	25	56	25	23
23.3	LARNE	27	43	27	25
24.3	LARNE HARBOUR	29	57	29	57

percent cut-off the whole way, with variations in the regulator opening. We went over Greenisland summit at 50½mph and there was little restraint on the coast section afterwards. Some time would be lost through a permanent way check through Whitehead tunnel, and this our driver was determined to make up. We passed Carrickfergus at 69mph, tore round the curves besides the sea at 66mph, and after the Whitehead slack I was given a good sample of the 'one wheel' technique at Magheramorne! We arrived at Larne Harbour dead on time. Exhilarating memories indeed.

CHAPTER 14

Great Southern: Climax of the Queens

W. H. Morton succeeded J. R. Bazin as Chief Mechanical Engineer of the Great Southern in 1929, and he continued the painful process of trying to make something worthwhile out of the Watson 4-6-0s. It was a difficult time economically, because the great worldwide slump was setting in, and traffic did not really justify the keeping in commission of ten fairly large 4-6-0 express locomotives, quite apart from the three mixed traffic 4-6-0s of Bazin's own design. So as briefly mentioned in Chapter 3 the drastic step was taken of scrapping the pioneer Watson 4-6-0 No 400 in 1929, and two more of them, Nos 404 and 408, in 1930. The last-mentioned was one of those built to use saturated steam. There was every reason to economise in fuel consumption, and maintenance charges, and to secure better utilisation from the big locomotives. Coal was an increasing problem. Although the Great Southern imported Welsh coal of good calorific value, by the time it arrived at the Irish sheds after mechanical handling at ports and during shipping much of it was reduced to no more than dust. The improved working of No 402 with two cylinders and long-lap, long-travel valves not only reduced consumption, but with a softer blast lessened the amount that was thrown out of the chimney unburned.

When Morton obtained authority to rebuild two more of the 4-cylinder 4-6-0s in the same way as No 402 had been treated, he attempted to secure even better coal consumption by use of Caprotti valve gear, instead of Walschaerts. Messrs Beardmore & Co of Glasgow had obtained a British licence to manufacture this gear, and successful applications of it had been made to four-cylinder 4-6-0 locomotives of the LMS and the LNER. On the former it was applied to 10 out of 20 locomotives of the Claughton Class that had been rebuilt with larger boilers, while on the LNER it was fitted on two ex-Great Central 4-6-0s of the Lord Faringdon Class. The last-mentioned could not be regarded as among the most successful of GCR locomotives, having a reputation for heavy coal consumption, and steaming that was not too reliable. The fitting of Caprotti valve gear transformed them, and they were regularly used on one of the hardest and fastest turns of duty on the line, the 2.32am newspaper express between Marylebone and Leicester. On the LMS the rebuilt Claughtons, while showing a considerable advantage over the original locomotives with smaller boilers, had no significant improvement over the 10 large-boilered ones with Walschaerts gear, which at the time of rebuilding had new piston valves fitted having solid valve heads and six narrow rings, in place of the rather complicated Schmidt type of piston valve and rings with trick ports that had been standard on all superheated express locomotives of the former LNWR.

On the Great Southern Nos 401 and 406 were chosen for rebuilding in 1930, and as with the previous rebuild of No 402 in Bazin's time, they became virtually new locomotives. With new frames and new wheels, quite apart from the new cylinders and motion, there was little except the boiler and firebox left of the originals. Despite the poor state of the coal when it eventually arrived on their tenders, this much can be said of the 400 Class locomotives in their original condition: they would steam, and that was something! On Nos 401 and 406 the drive to the valve

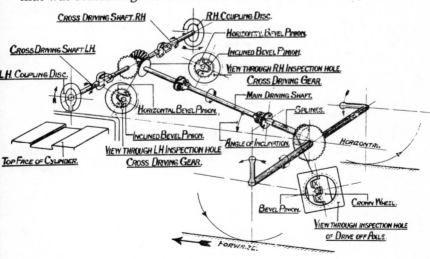

gear was taken from the leading coupled axle by a crown wheel and bevel pinion as shown in the accompanying diagram, with a transverse head drive to the rotary-cam gear boxes, arranged to pass clear under the relative low smokebox. The valves were of the earlier type as developed in Italy, being spring operated, whereas the later type, British-designed, were springless. The reversing wheel in the cab, arranged for left-hand drive, standard on the GSR since McDonnell's day, required only one full turn to adjust from full to mid gear. As originally fitted, the indicating plate was not marked for any cut-off short of 10 percent in either back or forward gear, and of this there is a tale to be told later.

In 1932 Morton had the honour of being chosen to succeed C. E. Riley as General Manager of the GSR and A. W. Harty, who had been Running Superintendent since the formation of the railway in 1925, was promoted to succeed him as Chief Mechanical Engineer. Harty carried on the process of rehabilitation of the 400 Class started by Bazin and continued by Morton, but with experience of the rebuilds Nos 401, 402 and 406 a cheaper form of conversion was evolved. First of all, to avoid the need for new wheels the piston stroke was shortened, using the new $19\frac{1}{2}$in cylinders, but fitting new covers that reduced the stroke to 26in. Then instead of having entirely new frames, in part necessitated by the increase of 6in between the leading coupled axle and the bogie, the frames were modified only at the front end, by rivetting on a longer and deeper frame plate section. Nos 403 and 405 were rebuilt in this way in 1933, and No 409 followed in 1935. The nominal tractive effort of these two locomotives was reduced only by the shorter piston stroke, making it 19,100lb against 20,600lb on Nos 401, 402 and 406. This left only No 407 as a four-cylinder locomotive in 1935.

Despite their other shortcomings no one could say that the Watson 4-6-0s were other than fast, but none of them was ever given an assignment equal to that put to the rebuilt No 402 on 20 March 1934, when the newly-appointed United States Minister to the Irish Free State arrived at Cobh and was conveyed by special train to Dublin. The train consisted of three coaches, including one of the palatial saloons of the former MGWR, a dining car, and a bogie brake van. Why it should have been thought necessary to convey the Minister to Dublin at record speed is not clear, but a 4-4-0 locomotive was used between Cobh and Cork, duly changed for the two-cylinder 4-6-0 No 402 at Glanmire station. The special was worked forward non-stop to Dublin at quite unprecedented speeds. The driver was the celebrated Mark Foley of Inchicore shed, with whom I had the pleasure of riding on the footplate some five years later. The run of March 1934 was not logged in the detail one would expect from Cecil J. Allen, but enough is available to stamp it as a most remarkable effort, particularly as the lengthy run was non-stop, with no chance of taking any additional supplies of water.

GSR CORK–DUBLIN
Special train: 3 coaches, 95 tons gross
Locomotive: 2-cylinder 4–6–0 No 402
Driver: M. Foley; fireman: P. Cornally

Distance miles	Locations	Time minutes	Average Speed mph
0.0	CORK	0	—
20.8	Mallow	24	52.0
58.4	LIMERICK JCN	60	62.7
78.8	Thurles	76	76.5
98.7	BALLYBROPHY	93	70.2
114.4	Maryborough	104	85.6
123.6	Portarlington	112	69.0
135.3	KILDARE	122	70.2
165.3	DUBLIN (KINGSBRIDGE)	147	72.0

The overall average speed was 67.5mph, including the very severe initial section from Cork to Mallow, while the average speed over the 106.9 miles from Limerick Junction to Dublin was 73.7mph. Even though the load was light by ordinary passenger train standards, if one includes the tender with the train No 402 was hauling 1.95 times its own weight, compared with *Flying Scotsman* on the first of the trial runs before the introduction of the Silver Jubilee made in that same year of 1934, when the load taken from King's Cross to Leeds was 2.3 times the weight of the locomotive. Even though the average speed on the LNER was higher the Irish run was a very notable performance.

My own first footplate runs on the Great Southern came in 1937, and on the down English Mail I was interested to find that our locomotive was to be No 401, the first of the Caprottis. The

191

load out of Dublin was 323 tons tare, and 345 tons full; for this we were provided with a pilot for the steep initial climb to Clondalkin, 1 in 114–84 for the first $1\frac{1}{2}$ miles to Inchicore, and then 1 in 138–169. The pilot was Coey 4-4-0 No 328 rebuilt and superheated. No 401 was worked hard at the outset, with regulator full open and 50 percent cut-off. Despite this, and the provision of an assisting locomotive we had reached no more than 42mph by Clondalkin. Directly we were up the bank the driver linked-up to 25 percent and changed the regulator setting to the first valve. This was the shortest cut-off I saw used on No 401. After Kildare, when we were unpiloted the driver never used less than 30 percent, and except south of Mallow making all his adjustments for power output on the regulator. As will be seen from the accompanying log we were making good time throughout. Although we had a tender full of what seemed little better than slack, the locomotive steamed well for quite three-quarters of the journey, but the fireman had some valuable help at each stopping station. To keep the dust down the water spray was liberally used, and this caused the slack to congeal, and refuse to trim forward. This was a well-known difficulty, and at each stopping station two men climbed aboard and helped the fireman to get coal forward. Had this procedure not been arranged, we could have been in some trouble.

The locomotive began to go really 'off the boil' after Limerick Junction, and on the racing descent from Knocklong past Kilmallock the driver shut off steam completely, allowing it to 'roll' at 66mph when we might have been doing well over 70mph. And after the summit near Two Pot House signalbox, with pressure still below normal the locomotive was allowed to coast on the fine downhill stretch into Mallow, not exceeding 61mph. But our final station stop, and hard work by the fireman gave us practically full pressure again by the time we were ready to leave. We were going strong on the lengthy toilsome ascent towards Mourne Abbey, working in 45 percent cut-off and full regulator when adverse signals were sighted, and speed had dropped to 15mph before they cleared. This spoiled the climb of the hardest bank, but a fast descent towards Cork, with a top speed of $82\frac{1}{2}$mph enabled us to finish the run practically on time. It was a competent and efficient performance especially in view of the constant difficulties with the coal. This was helped, of course, by

GSR 7.00am DUBLIN–CORK (ENGLISH MAIL)
Loads: to Kildare 44 axles, 323/345 tons
to Maryborough 40 axles, 301/320 tons
to Cork 38 axles, 290/310 tons
Locomotives: 4–6–0 No 401 (Caprotti Valve gear)
Pilot to Kildare 4–4–0 No 328

Distance miles	Locations	Schedule minutes	Actual min sec	Speeds mph	Regulator opening	Cut-off %
0.0	DUBLIN (KINGSBRIDGE)	0	0 00			
1.5	Inchicore		4 35		Full	50
4.4	Clondalkin		10 10	42	1st Valve	25
—			pws			
5.5	Newbridge		35 13	66		
0.0	KILDARE	42	41 15			
6.6	Monasterevan		8 05	68/50½	1st Valve	30
0.9	MARYBOROUGH	26	23 30			
8.5	Mountrath		11 44	67	⅝	30
5.7	BALLYBROPHY	23	20 32			
2.1	Templemore		14 18	70½	½	30
—			pws	72/40		
9.9	THURLES	24	23 08			
8.6	Goulds Cross		10 45	70½	1st Valve	30
7.5	Grange		19 57	56	¾	30
0.4	LIMERICK JCN	25	23 53			
6.6	Emly		11 12	59	1st Valve	30
7.2	Kilmallock		21 57	66	SHUT	
2.3	CHARLEVILLE		27 25	51½	⅞	30
0.3	Buttevant		35 49	75	Full	30
4.2	*Two Pot House*		39 58	51½	SHUT	
7.6	MALLOW	45	44 25			
—			—	36	Full	45
—			sigs	16		
3.9	Mourne Abbey		7 18	—	Full	70/50
9.9	Rathduff		17 41	36	1st Valve	30
5.0	Blarney		22 02	82½		
9.6	*Kilbarry*		26 45	—		
0.8	CORK	29	29 30	—		

the provision of men to assist the fireman at every stopping station.

I fear I did not do full justice to my opportunities on this occasion. I was suffering from a heavy cold, and after the journey from Euston to Holyhead, the usual broken night's rest, and nearly four hours on the footplate I was somewhat jaded by the time we reached Cork. Furthermore I had next to scrape and wash off the incredible coating of grime that the dusty coal had plastered on my face and neck. But it was a beautiful day, and there were many locomotives on the shed just waiting to be photographed, so I bucked up and exposed a good deal of film. After lunch reaction set in, and when I learned that although the load of the return mail on which No 401 was to work was to be no more than 362 tons, against the maximum of 450 tons booked to these locomotives, and that a 4-4-0 locomotive working home was to be coupled on as pilot as far as Ballybrophy, I decided to ride in the train. Thus I missed the opportunity of seeing whether the Inchicore driver used any different technique in handling the Caprotti valve gear. Up that backbreaking initial incline out of Cork, with its two miles of 1 in 60, after emerging from that fearsome tunnel that one dives into straight off the platform end, and which continues on 1 in 78–64 for a full mile inside its blackness, we had a third locomotive to assist as far as Blarney – McDonnell 0-6-0 No 141, dating from 1881.

An account of my footplate experience on No 401 was published in the late autumn of 1937 and a friend of mine, L. T. Daniels, then on the staff of Caprotti Valve Gears Ltd, told me that they were so shocked at the way the locomotive was handled – albeit with apparently no adverse effect on its economy – that he went over to Ireland in the following year to instruct the drivers to handle the reversing gear in the way it is designed to be used. He found that owing to the hand wheel only having cut-off positions indicated up to 10 percent they had never known that it was possible to notch up as far as three percent. In fact many of the drivers said that he was putting the locomotive in reverse when he tried to show what could be done in that direction. He made the additional markings for 7, 5 and 3 percent, but although they did a great deal of remarkably good work with full regulator and short cut-offs with both Nos 401 and 406 the drivers themselves retained a strong inclination for half-open regulators and around 20 percent cut-off.

On my own return trip with the English Mail, beyond noting that the three locomotives sustained a speed of 24mph on the 1 in 60 gradient out of Cork, I did not take a great amount of detail until we detached the pilot at Ballybrophy. There the load was reduced to 360 tons. The first short section to Maryborough is easily-timed, but I have tabulated the concluding non-stop run to Dublin. The start is on slightly favourable gradients, but after Monasterevan there is a four-mile ascent at 1 in 180 to Kildare, where speed fell to 41mph. After passing Curragh signalbox the gradients are easily downhill for the rest of the way into Dublin. Here we made some good speed, and finished just over four minutes early.

The final development of the 400 Class 4-6-0 locomotives was due to E. C. Bredin, who succeeded A. W. Harty as Chief Mechanical Engineer in 1937. Apart from a short period in his early training years, the new chief had spent his entire career since 1907 in the service of the GS&WR and later the GSR and had been Works Manager at Inchicore since 1921. The original boiler fitted to the 400 Class, good as it had proved, was thought capable of improvement, and in the autumn of 1937 an enlarged version was fitted to Nos 403 and 405.

GSR 400 CLASS BOILERS

Details	Standard up to 1937	K class on No 403 & 405
Barrel: maximum diameter	5ft 2$\frac{3}{4}$in	6ft 0in
length	14ft 1$\frac{3}{4}$in	14ft 5$\frac{1}{2}$in
Firebox: length	8ft 0in	8ft 6$\frac{1}{2}$in
' width between frame plates	4ft 5$\frac{1}{2}$in	4ft 5$\frac{1}{2}$in
Grate area	28sq ft	28sq ft
Tubes, 1$\frac{3}{4}$in dia	168	183
Flues	24	24
Plate thickness	$\frac{5}{8}$in	$\frac{11}{16}$in
Heating surfaces.		
Tubes	1595sq ft	1606sq ft
Firebox	158sq ft	171sq ft
Superheater	366sq ft	350sq ft
Total	2119sq ft	2127sq ft
Weight of locomotive	73.75 tons	75.5 tons
Weight of adhesion	54.85 tons	56.35 tons

Apart from the increase in diameter of the barrel, which provided space for more tubes, the principal difference was in the design of the firebox, which had a sloping throat plate, and the length between the tube plates was reduced to 13ft 9in. Thus although there were many more tubes than in the 400 Class standard the tube heating surface was little more. The firebox heating surface was considerably increased. The thickness of the boiler plates was increased from $\frac{5}{8}$in to $\frac{11}{16}$in to permit of an increase boiler pressure to 225lb/sq in if desirable at some future time. It will have been noted that the locomotives originally fitted with the K Class boiler were those having 26in piston stroke.

With business improving towards the end of the 1930s and the loading of the mail trains constantly on the increase Mr Bredin received authority to build an entirely new class of three-cylinder 4-6-0 express passenger locomotive, which eventually took shape in 1939 as the Queen Class – without question the most distinctive and outstanding ever to run the rails in Ireland. With a nominal tractive effort at 85 percent boiler pressure of 33,000lb, and a locomotive weight in working order of 84 tons, it was inevitable that comparisons of the basic dimensions should be made with two British designs that seemed to correspond closely, namely the Royal Scot of the LMS, and the Lord Nelson of the Southern. It is also interesting to set alongside the boiler proportions the valve setting, both of which can have so marked an effect on the performance. On the face of it one could imagine there would be very little difference, and my own experience on the footplate and otherwise certainly showed this to be so. There were nevertheless some marked differences in the draughting arrangements at the front end. The Royal Scot had a single orifice blastpipe, and a chimney of 1ft 3in internal diameter – most unusually parallel throughout. The Lord Nelson originally had a chimney that also had a minimum diameter of 1ft 3in, but it tapered outwards in approximate conformity with the issuing jet of exhaust steam. This was considered to be the ideal shape for good steaming though in practice, before the Bulleid modifications were made, the Nelsons were not the most free-steaming of locomotives. The Scots on the other hand were excellent.

On the GSR Queens Bredin introduced what I believe to be a unique arrangement. He used a twin-orifice blastpipe and double chimney, but segregated the exhausts from the inside and outside cylinders. The one inside cylinder exhausted through the forward blastpipe, while the two outside cylinders exhausted through the rearward one. The twin exhausts provided the valuable entraining action of the normal form of double chimney, and although the total volume of steam passing through the two blastpipes was not equal, the steaming was very free. The Queens were massively-built. Bredin had been in a senior position at Inchicore throughout the time when trouble was being experienced with the Watson four-cylinder 4-6-0s, and he specified frames $1\frac{1}{4}$in thick for his own. By contrast the Lord Nelson had only 1in thick frames, and the Royal Scot $1\frac{1}{8}$. Only one locomotive had been completed by the time Great Britain declared war on Nazi Germany, the celebrated No 800 *Maeve*.

THREE OUTSTANDING 4–6–0s

Railway Class	LMS Royal Scot*	Southern Lord Nelson†	GSR Queen
Nominal tractive effort (85% boiler pressure)	33,150lb	33,500lb	33,000lb
Cylinders: Number	3	4	3
diameter	18in	$16\frac{1}{2}$in	$18\frac{1}{2}$in
stroke	26in	26in	28in
Coupled wheel diameter	6ft 9in	6ft 7in	6ft 7in
Boiler:			
Heating surfaces			
Tubes	1892sq ft	1795sq ft	1670sq ft
Firebox	189sq ft	194sq ft	200sq ft
Superheater	416sq ft	376sq ft	468sq ft
Grate area	31.2sq ft	33.0sq ft	33.5sq ft
Distance between tube plates	14ft 6in	14ft 2in	14ft 6in
Boiler pressure	250lb/sq in	220lb/sq in	225lb/sq in
Motion:			
Diameter of piston valves	9in	8in	9in
Max valve travel	$6\frac{3}{16}$in	$6\frac{1}{2}$in	$6\frac{3}{4}$in
Steam lap	$1\frac{7}{16}$in	$1\frac{5}{8}$in	$1\frac{1}{2}$in
Exhaust clearance	Nil	Nil	Nil
Lead	$\frac{1}{4}$in	$\frac{1}{4}$in	$\frac{3}{16}$in
Total locomotive weight	84.9 tons	83.5 tons	84 tons
Adhesion factor	4.22	4.15	4.3

*Original type   †with Bulleid modifications

As completed in 1939 this anglicised version of the name was used, though rendered on the nameplates in Erse characters, but it was subsequently changed to *Maedhbh*. The other two locomotives completed later in 1939, were Nos 801 *Macha* and 802 *Tailte*.

Maeve, as I knew it in 1939, was a lovely engine. It was still under fairly close observation from Inchicore when Mr Bredin gave me the privilege of some footplate passes; it was not a moment too soon because three weeks later we were at war. Apart from that, the traffic department evidently had the utmost confidence in the ability of the new locomotives, because for the summer service of 1939 they tabled some striking acceleration of the mail trains. Previously, as noted earlier in this chapter, the departure of the down train had been 7.00am from Kingsbridge, but as the postal vans and the through carriages from Dun Laoghaire had to be worked round the junction line and direction reversed at Islandbridge Junction there was not a great deal of time to spare, the GSR mail sometimes getting away late after making the connections. The new timing was for a 7.15am departure, but with an arrival in Cork at 10.48am instead of 10.55am an acceleration of 22 minutes. A demonstration run was made on 17 July with the new locomotive, and the total gains on the new schedule amounted to eight minutes, showing a gain of 30 minutes on the previous timing. On my own run with No 401 in 1937 the total gain to by the locomotive was $9\frac{1}{4}$ minutes on the old schedule. In the course of the demonstration run of 17 July it was reported that a maximum speed of 92mph was attained.

When making arrangements for my own trip the GSR advised me that because of heavy summer traffic the mail would be running in two parts, with the through section from Dun Laoghaire forming the second part. So I crossed from Holyhead by the day boat on the previous day and stayed the night in Dublin. With the first part of the train, by a coincidence *Maeve* had exactly the same load on each section that I had noted with No 401 two years earlier, and it just romped away, taking no assistance out of Kingsbridge into the bargain. Our total gains on the *new* schedule amounting to $11\frac{1}{4}$ minutes. Twice we attained 'even time' from the start, near Grange signalbox in the relatively short run from Thurles to Limerick Junction, and again before Mallow, where we made a start-to-stop run of 37 minutes 48 seconds over the 37.6 miles from Limerick Junction. It was on this stretch that we attained the highest speed of the trip, 82mph near Kilmallock. On each stretch the locomotive was being worked in 20 percent cut-off, mostly with the regulator about one-half open.

The most impressive performance was reserved for the heavily-graded final section from Mallow to Cork, which begins with the seven-mile climb at 1 in 125–140 to Milepost 151½. Here *Maeve* accelerated to some effect with regulator full open and 22 percent cut-off, the speed rapidly rising until we topped the summit at no less than 52mph. Then after touching 77mph at Blarney we made a very cautious descent of the precipitous last 3½ miles into Cork, to arrive three minutes early, in the unprecedented time of only 24 minutes for that very difficult 20.8 miles from Mallow. Our total running time on the journey from Dublin amounted to 181 minutes 47 seconds, an average of 54.8mph, with the load reduced from the initial 340 tons to 305 tons south of Maryborough. The locomotive steamed very freely throughout, and the riding was luxuriously smooth and quiet.

I was feeling vastly better than on my earlier visit to Cork, and once I had cleaned up the turn-round time before the departure of the up mail at 4.05pm passed quickly and delightfully. In the early afternoon I learned that an eastbound, transatlantic liner, had landed a considerable number of passengers by tender at Cobh, all bound for Dublin, and the extra stock required for their accommodation made up the heaviest load that any locomotive had ever been called upon to tackle single-handed out of Cork. It was significant that the passenger stop at Blarney had been cut out in the new timetable. Previously, with the mail regularly needing assistance out of Cork that stop had been a case of making a virtue out of necessity. *Maeve* and its two sisters were evidently not expected to require assistance, and for all the traffic that it picked up a stop at Blarney would henceforth not be worthwhile. All the same, it is doubtful if such a load as I was to witness on that Saturday afternoon was contemplated when the locomotive department decided to dispense with a banking engine when a Queen was working the mail. On that day the senior locomotive authorities at Cork were as excited as the keenest amateur enthusiast to see what *Maeve* would do with the huge train. I recalled the time two years previously when for a 390-ton train we had three locomotives: a McDonnell 0-6-0, a rebuilt and superheated 4-4-0, and Caprotti 4-6-0 No 401. Now, *Maeve* was going to take 450 tons on its own.

So great was the interest that the District Locomotive Superintendent, the shedmaster at Glanmire, and a local running inspector all joined us on the footplate; together with a young engineer from Inchicore works, the crew, and myself this made a grand total of seven in the cab. I was pleased to find that our driver was Mark Foley of Inchicore shed, who had made the record run of March 1934 referred to earlier. He had a splendid young fireman named Ryan, and all concerned were evidently out to make the most of what promised to be a great occasion. The start was terrific. Full regulator almost at once, and nothing less than 50 percent cut-off once we were under way in that shocking tunnel. But there was no slipping, and even *Maeve* roused the echoes once we were into the open, and climbing steadily at 22mph to 23mph on the 1 in 60. Moreover, with the 450-ton train it made slightly faster time than the three locomotives on my previous trip had made with 390 tons. Then on topping the bank, and having the regulator eased back briefly, the valve stuck and it could not be opened again. Foley tugged at the handle with all his might, and eventually he had to link up while climbing at 1 in 178 before it could be freed. As a consequence speed fell to 30mph on a gradient where we would have been doing nearer 45mph, and $3\frac{1}{2}$ minutes was lost on schedule to Mallow. Here our visitors from Cork left us, and we took with us their good wishes for the rest of the journey.

At first it seemed as though we might need it. The next section to Limerick Junction is very sharply timed – a little too sharply, I thought, with only 43 minutes for the 37.9 miles, particularly as time had to be allowed for running past and setting back into that extraordinary station layout. With a train of this magnitude it was astonishing that the time between the first stop and arrival in the platform took only 2 minutes 26 seconds; but nevertheless to keep strict time would have meant making a start-to-stop run from Mallow to the east end of Limerick Junction in $40\frac{1}{2}$ minutes, 56.2mph, beginning with a four-mile climb at 1 in 151 right off the platform end at Mallow. I have no doubt it would have been easy enough for *Maeve* with the normal load of the mail, 350 to 400 tons, but it was another matter with 450 tons. Up the initial bank we accelerated to $38\frac{1}{2}$mph and then on the continuation to Knocklong, undulating but with a definitely rising tendency, we made an average of around 60mph until adverse signals at Emly pulled us down to 20mph. This check cost us at least three minutes, but even without it I think we should have dropped $1\frac{1}{2}$ to two minutes on that sharp schedule. And we were not 'through the wood' even yet. Watching fireman Ryan's work and the kind of coal he was having to deal with, I had been wondering how soon it would be before we began to lose pressure; sure enough it came on the next section, where careful nursing of the boiler, with easier steaming, rallied the boiler, but involved us in a loss of a further $2\frac{3}{4}$ minutes. But this was the end of our troubles.

Up to our arrival in Ballybrophy the locomotive could be debited with a loss of $4\frac{1}{4}$ minutes on schedule, plus another $3\frac{1}{2}$ minutes from that episode with the regulator, after that monumental start out of Cork. But *Maeve* and her crew covered themselves with glory in the final dash for Dublin, in which the locomotive gained $7\frac{1}{2}$ minutes on the schedule time of 58 minutes for the 50.9 miles from Maryborough into Kingsbridge, despite a permanent way slowing at Portarlington. The log of this final stage of a memorable run makes an interesting comparison with that of the Caprotti 4-6-0 No 401. The Queen ran magnificently on this section, working in 20 percent cut-off, except in taking the 1 in 180 climb to Kildare, where 25 percent was used. The driver had the main valve of the regulator open, though the position of the handle indicated no more than about half open. But if *Maeve* was anything like some of its contemporaries on the other side of the Irish Sea the amount of throttling would be very small and I would judge that the steam chest pressure would be nearly if not quite 200lb/sq in. It was a joyous finish to my journeys in Ireland before the second world war, and I was only sorry that my need to continue with the boat train connection to Dun Laoghaire precluded my staying longer on the footplate of *Maeve* in the congenial company of Driver Foley and Fireman Ryan.

I shall not forget what could be called the epilogue of this trip, and indeed of this entire varied odessey on Irish railways. I was bound for Holyhead and home, and so were quite a lot of other

GSR 6.40pm MARYBOROUGH–DUBLIN
Load: 337 tons tare, 360 tons full
Locomotive: 4–6–0 No 401 (Caprotti Valve gear)

Distance miles	Location	Schedule minutes	Actual min sec		Speeds mph
0.0	MARYBOROUGH	0	0	00	—
9.2	Portarlington		12	42	63½
14.3	Monasterevan		17	36	59
18.5	*Cherryville Jcn*		22	09	48
20.9	KILDARE	26	25	31	41
23.2	*Curragh*		28	48	50/46
25.4	Newbridge		30	58	69
33.0	Sallins		37	49	64
37.8	Straffan		42	03	70½
40.9	Hazelhatch		44	44	72
44.1	Lucan		47	36	65/71
46.5	Clondalkin		49	45	68
49.4	Inchicore		52	35	—
50.2	*Islandbridge Jcn*		53	48	—
50.9	DUBLIN (KINGSBRIDGE)	60	55	43	—

GSR MARYBOROUGH–DUBLIN
Load: 421 tons tare, 450 tons full
Locomotive: 3-cylinder 4–6–0 No 800 *Maeve*
Driver: Foley; Fireman: Ryan

Distance miles	Location	Schedule minutes	Actual min sec		Speeds mph
0.0	MARYBOROUGH	0	0	00	—
3.9	*Milepost 47*		5	52	60
7.9	*Milepost 43*		9	42	67
—			pws		
9.2	Portarlington		11	03	40
14.3	Monasterevan		15	57	67
16.9	*Milepost 34*		18	27	62½
18.5	*Cherryville Jcn*		20	02	56
20.9	KILDARE	25	22	51	50
23.4	*Milepost 27½* (Curragh)		25	43	57/54½
25.4	Newbridge		27	38	79
—			—		70½
33.0	Sallins	38	33	57	72/69
37.8	Straffan		37	56	75
40.9	Hazelhatch		40	28	76½
44.1	Lucan		43	11	69
46.5	Clondalkin		45	10	72
48.4	*Milepost 2½*		—		72½
49.4	Inchicore		47	43	—
50.9	DUBLIN (KINGSBRIDGE)	58	50	35	—

Net time 50 min

people! When I made my way rearwards from the locomotive I found that the boat train portion we had conveyed, some of it right through from Cobh, was absolutely packed, and the returning holiday makers had no small difficulty in making room for a dirty fellow in overalls to find some way of getting into the train. In those jumpy days, when there were almost as many bomb incidents as there are today, there were suspicious looks too. It was not until I got on to the boat at Dun Laoghaire and saw my face in a mirror that I realised why; for after a spell of that dusty GSR coal on *Maeve's* footplate, I was again indescribably filthy. But in saying farewell to Ireland I had the feeling that it would be many years before I came back again, and so it turned out – eight years in fact, and then at a time when the whole complexion of railways, not only in Ireland but all over the world, was changing dramatically.

Index

Achill Sound, 51
Adavoyle, 163, 172
Antrim, 113
Armoured train, 133
Athlone, 48, 57
Atmospheric line, 130

Ballycastle, 128
Ballymena, 126 et seq
Ballyshannon, 116
Belfast:
  Gt Victoria St, 170–1
  Queens Quay, 95, 99
  York Road, 175
Blarney, 44, 199
Boyne viaduct, 80
Bray, 131, 135, 152
Burtonpoint, 123, 125

Caprotti valve gear, 188 et seq
Civil War damage, 27, 40–1, 52
Clifden, 51
Cobh (Queenstown), 16, 19, 23
Coleraine, 114
Colours, loco:
  County Donegal, 119–20
  Great Northern, 170
  Midland GW, 55, 57, 62
  NCC, 103, 111
Cookstown, 111
Cork, 19, 23, 38, 42, 137, 147
Cushendall, 126

Dalkey, 129
Dividends (pre-group), 12
Donaghadee, 94
Donegal, 115
Downpatrick, 94, 95
Drogheda, 80, 88
Dublin:
  Amiens St, 83, 136, 153
  Broadstone, 21, 29, 49, 57, 137, 143, 154
  Harcourt St, 130, 151, 153
  Junctions, 154
  Kingsbridge, 198, 201
  North Wall, 49, 56, 153
  Westland Row, 131, 135, 137, 143, 151, 153

Dundalk, 32, 79, 83, 163, 170
Dun Laoghaire (Kingstown), 16, 34, 56, 129, 135, 140, 170

Engineers:
  Atock, M., 29, 49, 52
  Bazin, J. R., 27–8, 31, 42, 144, 188
  Bredin, E., 9, 194
  Clifford, C., 15, 31, 77, 83
  Coey, R., 26, 34, 149
  Cronin, R., 34, 133
  Crosthwait, H. W., 26
  Crosthwait, J. L., 24, 25, 34, 98
  Cusack, E., 51, 60
  Daniels, L. T., 193
  Glover, G. T., 15, 25, 31, 77 et seq 163, 168
  Harty, A. W., 31, 190, 194
  Howden, G. B., 9, 32, 163, 171
  Joynt, W., 26
  Livesay, R. M., 118
  Malcolm, Bowman, 15, 25, 33, 102 et seq
  Maunsell, R. E. L., 15, 21, 26, 37, 43, 145
  McDonnell, A., 16, 149
  Miller, R. G., 25–6, 97
  Morton, W. H., 20, 25, 29, 31, 42, 60, 144, 151, 188, 190
  Patrick, M., 176
  Wallace, W. K., 33
  Watson, E. A., 21, 25–6, 37, 151
  Wild, G. H., 34, 140, 147
Ennis, 66

Galway, 19, 48, 51, 57, 135, 156
Glenagalt, 73
Goraghwood, 81, 163, 166
Greenisland, loop, 106, 175
Grouping, Irish, 28

Kildare, 14, 38, 47, 192
Kilrush, 66

Light Railways, Acts, 64
Limerick Junction, 42, 47, 200
Listowel, 75
Londonderry, 81, 115, 124, 125

Index

Locomotives:
Belfast & County Down, 95 *et seq*
  4–4–2 tank, 97 *et seq*
  4–6–4 tank, 98
  Loco stock, 100
Belfast & Northern Counties narrow gauge, 126 *et seq*
Cork, Bandon & South Coast 4–6–0T, 147
County Donegal, 117 *et seq*
Dublin & South Eastern, 132–9
  Civil War casualties, 138
  2–6–0 goods, 140
  Names, 133–5
Great Northern:
  Simple 4–4–0s, 78 *et seq*, 162
  Compound 4–4–0s, 158 *et seq*, 164–8
  Rebuilt 4–4–0s, 168–173, 178
  4–4–2 tanks, 83
Great Southern:
  Standardisation, 144
  Woolwich 2–6–0s, 145–6, 155
  2–6–2 tank, 146
  New numbering, 149
  0–6–2 tank, 153
  Caprotti 4–6–0s, 188, 195
  The Queens, 4–6–0, 196 *et seq*
Great Southern & Western:
  Ivatt 4–4–2 tank, 63
  4–4–0 '60' class, 46, 150
  4–4–0 Coey, 46–7, 151–2
  4–4–0 Maunsell, 21, 26, 39
  4–6–0 '400' class, 21, 27, 37, 40 *et seq*, 190–2
  4–6–0 '500' class, 43, 146
  4–8–0 tank, 148
Irish 4–4–0s of 1920, 22
Listowel & Ballybunion, 75
Londonderry & Lough Swilly, 121 *et seq*
Midland Great Western:
  Atock's 2–4–0s, 49, 59
  'Connemara' class, 51, 156
  2–4–0 rebuilding, 151
  4–4–0s, (Cusack), 20–1, 51, 57, 58
  Kylemore, 30, 59, 62
  Loco stock in 1925, 61
Names:
  County Donegal, 120
  Dublin & South Eastern, 133–5
  Great Northern, 169
  Midland Great Western, 50, 51, 59
  Northern Counties, 109–110
Northern Counties (LMS):
  Compounds, 102 *et seq*, 110 *et seq*
  4–4–0 engine loadings, 106
  Superheater 4–4–0s, 103, 182–3
  2–6–0s, 176 *et seq*
Schull and Skibbereen, 74

Tralee and Dingle, 68–70
West Clare, 67–8
Logs of Runs:
Great Northern:
  Dublin–Dundalk, 84
  Dundalk–Belfast, 86
  Belfast–Dundalk, 85
  Dundalk–Dublin, 87
  Dundalk–Goraghwood, 114
  Portadown–Dundalk (84), 165
  Dublin–Dundalk (84), 167–8
  Drogheda–Dublin (85), 168
  Belfast–Dublin (173), 173
Great Southern:
  Cork–Dublin (402), 191
  Dublin–Cork (401), 195
  Maryborough–Dublin (401), 202
  Maryborough–Dublin (800), 202
Great Southern & Western:
  Dublin–Mallow (401), 41
  Dublin–Cork (502), 45
  Thurles–Dublin 4–4–0 (332), 47
Midland Great Western:
  Galway–Dublin, 58
  Mullingar–Dublin, 61
Northern Counties (LMS):
  Belfast–Antrim (2–4–0), 112
  Belfast–Portrush (96, 90, 79), 181
  Portrush–Belfast (4, 96), 186
  Belfast–Larne Harbour (62, 81), 187

Mallow, 27, 40, 200
Mileage, pre-grouping, 12
Mullingar, 21, 48, 55, 60, 155

Newcastle (Co Down), 94–5

Passing loops layout, NCC, 176
Personalities:
Ahrons, E. L., 48, 52
Aspinall, Sir John, 31, 149
Forbes, E., 117 *et seq*
Hunt, H., 122
Keogh, M. F., 29
Paget, Sir C. W., 174
Pim, F. W., 133
Pim, James, 130
Speir, Major M. S., 9, 174 *et seq*
Tatlow, Joseph, 13, 30, 121
Willox, W. A., 175

Roaring Water Bay, 64, 74
Rosslare, 131
Royal trains, 58

Services, train:
Accelerations, GNR, 161 *et seq*
Accelerations, NCC, 175 *et seq*
American mails, via Queenstown, 16
Belfast & Co Down, commuters, 95–9

Index

County Donegal, 116
Dublin & South Eastern, with packet sailings, 135–8
Dublin & South Eastern, commuters, 143
English mail connections, 14
Great Northern,
  Main line, 79–80
  Dublin–Howth, 83
Great Southern, English mail, 43
Killarney Express, 55
Larne boat trains, 185
Lough Swilly, 123 *et seq*
Midland Great Western Limited Mail, 21, 49, 56, 60, 155
Narrow gauge boat train, 127
North Atlantic Express, 178, 182
NCC Cookstown–Derry Central, 111–14
Portrush Flyer, 178, 183
Post Office required timings, 19
Slip coaches, on GNR, 88, 92
Tralee & Dingle cattle specials, 70, 73

Waterford Mail, 131
  West Clare, 66
Sligo, 48, 55, 135
Strabane, 115
Stranorlar, 115–16, 120

Triple heading from Cork, 193

Warrenpoint, 81, 163
Waterford, 19, 131, 152
Westport, 48, 51
Wexford, 131
Works, railway:
  Armstrong–Whitworth, 24, 39
  Broadstone, 29, 50, 145, 155
  Crewe, 25
  Doncaster, 28
  Dundalk, 31
  Grand Canal St, 147
  Hunslet Engine Co, 66
  Inchicore, 15, 23, 65, 146, 155
  Kerr, Stuart, 73
  Woolwich Arsenal, 144